LESLIE DYANNE

I Am the
Whisper
of the
Wind

My Journey
from
Darkness to Light

Foreword by Marci Shimoff

Edited by: Amy Delcambre
Cover Design by: Kristina Edstrom

EMPOWER
P   R   E   S   S

An Imprint for GracePoint Publishing (www.GracePointPublishing.com)

GracePoint Matrix, LLC
624 S. Cascade Ave, Suite 201, Colorado Springs, CO 80903
www.GracePointMatrix.com   Email: Admin@GracePointMatrix.com
SAN # 991-6032

A Library of Congress Control Number has been requested and is pending.

ISBN: (Paperback) 978-1-961347-75-5
eISBN: 978-1-961347-76-2

Books may be purchased for educational, business, or sales promotional use.
For bulk order requests and price schedule contact:
Orders@GracePointPublishing.com

Wrinkled Eyelids

Don't cry, he said.

You will have wrinkled eyelids.

My eyelids *are* wrinkled.

I could not stop crying.

Day after day.

Doesn't anyone see?

Doesn't anyone hear?

Doesn't anyone care?

No, there is not just one of me.

There are thousands and thousands of me

littering every society

all with wrinkled eyelids.

This book is dedicated to all the women of the world who have

Wrinkled Eyelids

Table of Contents

Foreword... vii

Introduction ix

Part I: The Enveloping Darkness...................................1

   Chapter 1: In the Beginning 3

   Chapter 2: Outdoor Sanctuaries............................9

   Chapter 3: Family Secrets 15

   Chapter 4: A Not-So-Chosen Path 27

   Chapter 5: Married Life...................................37

   Chapter 6: First Time 53

   Chapter 7: It Is Time to Leave............................61

   Chapter 8: Finding My Truth 71

Part II: Into the Light...81

   Chapter 9: A New Life 83

   Chapter 10: Who Am I? 95

   Chapter 11: My Spiritual Journey 103

   Chapter 12: Godwinks.....................................115

   Chapter 13: Lessons from My Daughter 123

   Chapter 14: Angels Everywhere............................141

   Chapter 15: Emissary for God 149

   Chapter 16: A Few Final Musings...........................155

Poetic Works By Leslie Dyanne.....................................161

My Grateful Acknowledgments 177

Resources...181

About the Author..183

Foreword

Ask anyone what they want most in life and they will likely answer, "To be happy." But what does happiness mean, exactly?

That question, and my own desire to be truly happy after suffering from depression early in my life, led me on a quest. I interviewed top researchers in the field of positive psychology and spoke with more than 100 of the happiest people in the world. Their findings, experiences, and revelations are the basis of my best-selling book, *Happy For No Reason*.

Through this exploration, I saw all too clearly how often we look to our outer circumstances to dictate our level of happiness. We eagerly await the arrival of our perfect home, our ideal loving partner or the job that comes with a high-paying salary. Most of us are convinced that when these things arrive, then we'll truly be happy. We're caught in a perpetual state of waiting, putting off our happiness until the outside world gives us what we think we need or want.

Based on that perspective of happiness, anyone looking at the surface of Leslie Dyanne's life would assume that she was happy: she was beautiful, she had a husband who had a thriving career and supported his family, she had a lovely home that she tended to with care, and she was the mother to two children whom she adored.

But those external details of her life didn't reflect what was really happening. From the time Leslie was born, her life was filled with neglect and abuse at the hands of her parents. The abusive experiences continued into her marriage until Leslie bravely chose to leave and forge a new life for herself.

One of the most important keys to living a happy and fulfilled life is to choose to be the hero of your life rather than a victim of the circumstances and events of life. Leslie could have easily fallen into victimhood given the abuse she experienced and the depression that came as a result of it. But, as you'll read in these pages, Leslie refused to allow these circumstances to define her. Instead, she took action—one small step at a time.

She started showing up more authentically in her life, forgave those who'd harmed her, cleared away old resentments, and leaned into trusting life. With each baby step, more and more opportunities opened for her.

This is an inspiring story of true transformation. Starting from a dark and wounded place, Leslie learned to unconditionally love herself and open to deep and sustainable happiness.

I've been blessed to know Leslie for the past few years, as she's a member of my *Year of Miracles* mentoring program. I've witnessed her life transform as she's healed her heart and experienced more love, connection, and joy as a result.

It's my hope that as you read these pages, you feel inspired to look to the true source of happiness within yourself. One thing I know for sure is that it's beating within your own heart.

With love and happiness,

Marci Shimoff
Number 1 *New York Times* Best Selling Author of
Happy for No Reason, Love For No Reason,
and *Chicken Soup for the Woman's Soul,*
Featured Teacher in *The Secret,*
& Founder of *Your Year of Miracles*

Introduction

When I first thought about writing this book, I thought I would write only about my spiritual journey into the light. Then, after telling a friend about my journey, I realized I had to tell the story from the beginning. If I did not tell it from where I started, you would not know how far I have come to be in this place of peace and love and light.

From the moment I was born, my mother made it clear to me that she never wanted me. I say "to me" because I do not think she let others know how she felt or how she treated me in private. I think she wanted people to think of her as a wonderful mother or maybe she was trying to convince herself that she was. Even though her treatment of me was cruel, every day when I took a nap, she polished my shoes. She dressed me in dresses that had to be ironed, and she put me in a clean dress when I woke up. Then she complained or boasted—I am not sure which it was—that she had done it every day.

Another story she told me over and over again was that my father would not buy a washing machine until they had saved up the money for it. Therefore, she had to scrub everything, including my diapers and all those dresses, on a washboard in the basement. She then had to carry the wet clothes up the basement stairs to hang them on the clothesline outside.

My pediatrician told my mother I needed to eat very nourishing foods, and my mother often reminded me that I refused to eat as a little child. As I was refusing to eat the expensive food she prepared for me, she was drooling over it because she and my father could only afford to eat hot dogs. I may have been offered lamb chops for dinner, worn two clean, beautifully ironed dresses every day, and my shoes may never have looked scuffed, but her words and treatment of me left deep scars that took years to erase.

How can one live without the love of a mother? I became a depressed and fearful child and then she criticized me for being so.

For years, these negative memories swirled through my mind, but now, I no longer dwell on those incidences. To write this book, I have had to revisit many of the things I no longer think about. I have had to remember things best forgotten. In remembering them, I realize how strong I am to have overcome them despite my mother constantly telling me how weak I was. For years I believed her, and now I know it was not true.

In telling my story, I want to be an inspiration to you, dear reader. I want you to know that you too have that same strength within you: the strength to step out of the darkness, to never think about it again, and to know it no longer has any power to harm you. I want you to know that you too can live in the light; live knowing you are surrounded by God's love. I want you to know you can soar with the angels and have the Holy Spirit as your guide, leaving fear and doubt behind.

I do not want to blame anyone, including myself. I think each person in my life has been put here for a purpose. God says in *Conversations with God* by Neale Donald Walsch that each person in our lives is here to help us remember who and what we really are.

Some people may say they are here to teach us lessons. God says they are here to help us remember what our soul already knows but what we, in this lifetime, have forgotten. Either way, I want to thank them. No matter how hard it was to live through some of these things, I would not be where I am today if I had not done so.

This is the story of my life's journey.

I now know I am the one in charge of the plot. My life began to really shift when I realized my thoughts were creating my story, and in order to change my story I had to change my thoughts. I became aware that when my thoughts were negative, I not only felt unhappy but I also attracted negative situations and people into my life. Conversely, when I think positive thoughts, I go out into the world with a loving heart, and I have the most amazing experiences with loving people. As I began to observe my thoughts, I was amazed to realize how many pessimistic, self-deprecating, grievous thoughts I was thinking. No wonder I was miserable! I had to have a strong desire to change my thoughts, and I had to make a very conscious effort to do so. My negative thoughts did not magically disappear when I decided I no longer wanted to think that way. I must constantly be vigilant and when I find my thoughts traveling in a negative direction, I stop myself and consciously think of something positive. Over time and with much practice it has become easier for me to think in a more positive way. Thinking of things I am grateful for is one approach I use to shift my thoughts because I cannot be grateful and despondent at the same time.

I have joined groups where I am with like-minded people who are also striving to change their manner of thinking. I started attending a Center for Spiritual Living where I was with others who were interested in learning how our thoughts create our reality. In addition, the computer is a wonderful tool as it enables me to listen to spiritual teachers from around the world.

I also realized I cannot always change my thoughts on my own. I often have to ask my angels for help. Recently, I was waiting at the Apple store to buy a new phone. When the salesman came out to get me, I said to myself, *Oh, please don't let this person be the one who is going to help me.* Immediately, I caught myself and said to the angels, *Please help me see this person differently.* And the shift in my perception was instantaneous, causing me to have a wonderful conversation with him as he helped me pick out a phone. I became genuinely interested in his story of how he, who is legally blind, is able to work in an Apple store. I had not realized he was blind when I first saw him.

My heart was profoundly touched when he said, "When I graduated from Blind School, I met this man who changed my life by offering me a job in this store." Before I left, we hugged, and the man told me I had been a blessing in his day. This would not have happened if I had not asked for help and shifted my way of viewing him, looking at him through the eyes of love instead of through disapproving eyes. Until I consciously began to pay attention to my thoughts, I did not realize their power in shaping my life.

Then there were the people in my life—my family and my friends—who were invested in having me be the person I had always been. I had a friend who did not know the first thing about me, yet she considered me her best friend. But because I never spoke my truth to her, I had allowed her to define me. I never corrected her when she told me who I was, and she was shocked when I started using my voice. We are no longer friends because she was friends with someone who did not really exist. I am not the person she had created me to be.

This was also true at home. As I began to uncover who I truly am and became stronger, my husband could no longer bully me into doing what he wanted me to do. The healthier I became mentally, the angrier he grew. When I realized this was happening, I knew I would never heal if I did not leave. So, in my own remembering of my truth, I had to leave some of my family and some of my friends who were too negative and toxic for me. My healing threatened them and their sense of security. I could not stay with them and heal. Their pull for me to stay in that place of misery was too great, and in order to have a chance to change my life, I had to go.

I have found friends and groups of people to replace them. People who are loving and kind, who allow me to be who I am, who cheer my achievements and comfort me in my sorrows. I am in no way saying what was right for me is necessarily right for you. Your journey is yours, and you must travel it in your way. You must find your own path, your own way of doing things.

I am sharing my story to show you it is possible to change and to grow. I want to be an example of how to live in a place where miracles are something that happen every day. I want you to know that you can transform your tears of sorrow into tears of joy. I was seventy years old before I started living in this place where I know I am supported and loved by the entire Universe. I have changed my life from one filled with fear and worry to a life of trusting that no matter what happens, it is happening for a reason—a divine reason. I may not see or understand the reason at the time, but I know that God has a plan for me.

When I just let go and allow, things happen that are more wonderful than I could ever have imagined. Maybe it does not unfold the way I think it should, but by believing, by living in a place of joy, I am open to having magical things flow into my life. In other words, it may not happen the way I think it should happen—it may happen in a far better way than I could have expected!

I could spend time wishing I had learned this years ago, but I have come to believe as the Bible says in Ecclesiastes 3:1: "To everything there is a season, and a time for every purpose under the sun." No, I do not waste my time wishing I had been younger when I learned these things. I just revel in the wonder, in the happiness, and in the joy that *this* is where I am living now.

I am, however, hoping that as you read this book you will learn this at a younger age and will have more of your life to live in joy rather than in sorrow. I cannot emphasize enough that God did not create us to be unhappy. We are the ones who make ourselves miserable. Isn't it almost comical when you think about that? Why do we continue to pick the path that leads to unhappiness when we could say, "No, I think I will go this way instead," and pick the path that leads to joy? Why do we spend so much time fighting with our loved ones, trying to convince them they are wrong and that we are right? When it comes down to it, does it really matter who is right and who is wrong? What is *right* and what is *wrong* anyway? It is just an opinion. What a freeing thing it was to let go of trying to convince others of what I believe. I now believe what I believe and allow others to believe what they believe, without judgment.

Yes, there are things that happen in life that bring us great sorrow. Things happen that we have no control over. I wrote this book from the perspective of abuse, but in talking about the book with other women, I have come to realize there are many reasons women cry and cannot stop crying. My thought is that when a tragedy occurs in our lives, we are more prepared to weather the storm if we start out in a place of love and peace and happiness. If a tragic event occurs when we are already in a place of misery, it may be the tipping point to push us over the edge into a very deep depression.

There may be some people who can change without much support from others, but I am not one of those people. I have needed professional help all along the way. I am still going to a counselor. With her support I am learning how to stay more consistently in the higher vibration of love and spiritual knowing—the knowing that I am constantly supported, helped, guided, and loved by the Universe.

I speak of God as *He* not because I believe Him to be an old man in the sky with an anger management problem, but because that is what I am comfortable with. I believe God is Love and only Love. We do not have to *do* anything to deserve His Love and we can do nothing to destroy it. If God is only Love how can this not be so? I do not think God judges us. He gave us free will. Why then would He punish us for something we chose to do? I believe God is present in everything—from the tiniest pebble to the highest mountain, from the closest stars to all the galaxies beyond, from the raindrop to the deepest ocean. He is a part of each and every one of us and each animal, insect, fish, and fowl. In other words, there is nothing He is not a part of.

If God is a part of everything and a part of us—then we must be a part of each other and a part of everything else also. I believe the Holy Spirit is the presence of God within us. Father Richard Rohr refers to the Holy Spirit as She—the feminine component of the Trinity. When I sit here thinking of this, it feels right. However, in the book I refer to the Holy Spirit as He. I am going to leave it that way. I cannot imagine God or the Holy Spirit cares how we refer to them. My beliefs are not rigid—they are fluid. This is the way I leave the door open for miracles to enter. I feel that if I were rigid in my beliefs, the door would be closed. God is a mystery. If He were a small easy Being to define, He would not be the all-loving, all-powerful God I believe in.

If the word *God* makes you uncomfortable, please substitute the word you feel comfortable with. There are many words for God just as there are many pathways to Him. If anything that I believe does not work for you, that is all right too. What feels right for me may not feel right for you, but please do not let my beliefs or my terminology obscure my message. As I have said many times throughout this book—I am not trying to convince you of anything. My hope is for you to find one thing that speaks to you. I think of it as finding one good recipe in a cookbook. That recipe may be the best thing you have ever made! I hope you find one gem here to excite you, to make you realize you deserve to live a safe, happy, joy-filled life overflowing with miracles.

Leslie Dyanne 2020

Part I:
The Enveloping
Darkness

Chapter 1

In the Beginning

I love the smell of new wood and the smell of tenpenny nails. My father and I are in the attic putting down a floor. I have been warned not to go too close to the edge because I could fall through the insulation and ceiling into the room below. I am my father's helper, a three-year-old with a hammer. I remember a loving father in the two places that were his domain—the attic and the basement. He made a swing for me in the basement and painted it green. He taught me how to swing myself by pumping my legs. I can remember the overwhelming feeling of elation when I accomplished what my father had so patiently taught me. No wonder to this day I love to swing.

Between the attic and the basement was my mother's domain, and my memories there tell a different story. As I sit here today with my eyes closed, I can feel my body shrink, my legs become short, my feet become small. I see myself sitting on an ottoman, my little legs not long enough for my feet to reach the floor. I have been told not to move, and I don't. My mother leaves the room secure in the knowledge that I will still be sitting there when she returns, no matter how long she is gone. She has told me she could leave for an hour or more (maybe forever), and I would not move. How proud she was, not of me but of her total control of me, a two- or three-year-old child. It was not until I had toddlers of my own that I asked myself: *What did my mother do to me to paralyze me with such fear?* Toddlers are *all* movement. That is their job.

In my forties, with the guidance of a therapist, I remembered some of the things my mother had done to cause me to be so deathly afraid of her. One of my memories was of her rubbing a dirty diaper in my face. When I had the memory, I could feel the feces in my nose; I could taste it in my mouth. I had no doubt it had happened because for years I had had a recurring nightmare. In the dream, I was trying to wash the feces off a baby, but I could never get the baby clean. I often dreamed about filthy bathrooms. After I had this memory and was helped by my psychiatrist to understand the implications of what had happened to me, I never had those nightmares again.

In my memory of being paralyzed with fear on my mother's ottoman, I see myself as the tiny child I was with my thin, wispy hair, sitting all alone in a semi-dark room. Maybe as I sat there, I thought about my father with his loving arms around me as he helped me hammer a nail into the new wood. *Did he know?*

All my life, my mother told me she did not want to marry my father, but her father and sister insisted. My mother and father had been high school sweethearts. Then he went off to war, flying fighter planes in the Pacific Theater, and my mother went on with her life, modeling in the Garment District in New York, starting nursing school at Wagner College, and dating the sailors and soldiers who were on leave in New York. When my father arrived home three or four years later, he expected to marry my mother. My grandfather told her she had to get married because he had already ordered the wedding cake. Her sister, who had first married at sixteen and was then married to her second of seven husbands, told her she was being a spoiled brat. So, my mother married my father on July 1, 1945. I was conceived on their honeymoon and was born nine months, nine days later on April 10, 1946, the very first year of the baby boomer generation. According to my mother, I sealed her fate. She was trapped, and I had been the one to trap her.

My mother was a truly beautiful woman. Her Jewish heritage gave her very dark hair and big, vividly blue eyes. But her disposition did not match her physical beauty. She was nasty and extremely cold—like a block of ice. She never hugged me. When I tried hugging her, she never put her arms around me. They hung limply by her sides. She was so unpleasant to my friends who came to visit me that they never wanted to come back to my house to play. I went to theirs instead.

Despite everything, my parents had three more children. My mother often did not speak to us for days. We never knew what we had done wrong, but of course as children we thought it was our fault. Now, I believe she was mad at my father, and we were just caught in the cross fire of silence.

I have a sister, Deborah, three years younger, another sister, Melanie, seven years younger, and a brother, David, ten years younger. Although each of us endured much childhood trauma, all my siblings say I was the one who received the brunt of it. I do not know if you can say one trauma is worse than another, but I do know I was a sad, withdrawn, frightened child. I was depressed and thought about suicide from the time I was a teenager until I received the help of that wonderful therapist when I was in my forties.

I was admitted to psychiatric hospitals twice, the first time in 1977 and the second time in 1990. If you are someone who has battled depression (and I do not use the word *battled* lightly for that is what it felt like to me—a battle that for years I was *not* winning), you know that horrible, deep, painful feeling. It is not only emotional and mental, but also physical. And when you are clinically depressed, it does not matter what you do to try to pull yourself out of it—everything is dark, completely devoid of light.

During the Korean War, my father was called back into the Navy and decided to make a career of it. At the age of five, I had to leave my loving grandparents, my very loving godmother, and my best friend, Rusty McGinnis, when we moved from Long Island to Virginia Beach, Virginia. My father was stationed aboard an aircraft carrier and was gone for six months at a time. Moving was devastating for me because I lost the support of those who cared about me, and I was alone with my mother and my little sister. People say children are resilient, but do they ever ask the children how they are feeling? I was miserable. My mother put me in a private kindergarten—Miss Barkley's.

Being in Miss Barkley's class was one of the first and only times I can remember feeling special. Even after all these years, I know she was one of those truly loving people who made each one of us feel that we were important and unique. She likely sensed how much I craved someone to notice me.

Each student had a Sucrets tin that was filled with tiny plastic animals. We used these to help us with simple arithmetic problems. This little metal box of animals made me feel very grown-up. I had been entrusted with what felt like a magical box. The top of our desks lifted up, and we stowed all our supplies inside. One of my vivid memories from my time with Miss Barkley is the day she brought a visitor to the class over to my desk to show her how neat and organized my things were. Now I realize that my desk was neat and organized because I was being raised by two rigid parents in a household where messes were forbidden.

Miss Barkley decided I was smart enough to go into first grade. Evidently, she did not confer with my mother about this, and when my mother found out, she was furious. She took me out of the school where I had been so happy and proud of myself, and I no longer attended kindergarten.

When I did go back to school, my first-grade teacher was an ogre. She hit our hands with a ruler when we did something she deemed wrong. I lived in such fear that when the teacher got mad at a girl for throwing up in the classroom, I started throwing up every morning after breakfast. I got it over with before going to school.

My father changed after he was back in the Navy. Gone was the loving father I remembered from the first five years of my life, and in his place was a person I did not know. I was accustomed to having him home every evening and on weekends, and now he was gone for six months at a time. He was a member of a macho group of fighter pilots, and he started to drink. This, along with his experiences in combat, started him down the long, dark road to becoming an alcoholic. No matter how drunk my father became, he thought of himself as an elegant, debonair man. In his mind he was never an alcoholic because he did not sneak into the pantry to drink as his parents, who were both alcoholics, had done. He was civilized and would have cocktails and hors d'oeuvres and a bottle of wine with dinner along with an after-dinner drink.

With my father back in the Navy, we moved from place to place every few years. I was always changing schools. Once, when I was in the second grade, I found myself standing in the corner in front of a classroom of students I had just met. What had I done? I do not recall, but I must have broken a rule I did not know about. That happened to me in more than one school. I was the new child in an unfamiliar environment with different rules. I never would have purposely broken a rule. I was too petrified!

When I started the sixth grade, I was entering my fourth elementary school. Every summer I was in high school, we moved, but by then it was not as terrifying for me to walk into a new classroom filled with students I did not know.

I always started the year with the wrong clothes. For example, if the girls wore poodle skirts, I had on a little plain dress. In those days it was definitely harder to fit in fashion-wise because girls were not allowed to wear pants.

Though my home and school often felt unsafe to me, my parents always rented houses in neighborhoods surrounded by wonderful places for a child to play and explore. These places were my sanctuaries, the places where I did feel safe. We never lived in a city or a big housing development. Wherever we lived, we were surrounded not by other houses but by woods or water. I often wonder— *would I have survived my childhood if I had not been able to spend my days outside reveling in the beauty of nature?*

Chapter 2

Outdoor Sanctuaries

When I was in the middle of the second grade and after living in Virginia Beach for two and a half years, we moved to Pensacola, Florida, into a neighborhood that was a young child's dream come true. It was an innocent time, years before mothers became fearful of letting their children out of their sight. Even though my sister Deborah had just turned five, and I had just turned eight, we were allowed to roam freely, to explore.

One day when I was exploring our new neighborhood alone, I came across a large strawberry patch. I thought I had discovered a treasure! Even all these years later, I remember thinking I had found something no one else knew about. As I reach down to pick a luscious red strawberry, a woman started yelling at me. It was her garden, and in my excitement, I had not noticed her sitting there. She so frightened me that I stood there wetting my pants as she yelled. Then I ran home.

Our house was on the water, a quiet bay. There were many old trees in the yard that gave us cool places to go on a hot day. My father hung a swing in the one in the front yard, a hammock between two on the side, and under a tree in the back, he built a large picket enclosure with a sign: Melanie's Acre. This created a safe place for my baby sister to play. It prevented her from wandering past the low brick wall onto the sandy beach and into the water. The mulberry tree next door could hold three or four hungry children, so we would perch on its branches, chattering like magpies while stuffing the fruit into our mouths until our stomachs started to ache. Another neighbor had pear trees, and we ate the fruit right off the trees while it was still hard and green, long before it was ripe. There were plenty of children to play with, and we were still young enough to all play together, the boys and the girls. We spent many hours running around with six-shooters in our holsters and cowboy hats on our heads.

But the water, oh, the water—to be able to run out of our back door in our bathing suits, through the backyard, onto the beach, and into the water—that was heaven! Usually, we swam off our neighbor's dock, jumping or diving off the end. The man who owned the dock was everyone's Uncle Joe, a grandfatherly man who always had time for all the neighborhood children. He helped us improve our swimming strokes and taught us how to dive by first holding us upside down by our ankles and dropping us into the water. We never tired of swimming. We stayed in the water until our fingers shriveled and our lips turned blue. If we got too cold, we rolled in the hot sand until we warmed up, then right back into the water we would go.

Then one day we went from joyful playing to witnessing a terrifying event. The day started out with our jumping off of the dock and splashing each other. We were playing games, simple games we had made up. We threw rocks into the water and dove for them. We tried sitting on the bottom, seeing who could stay under the longest. It was a carefree summer day when all we had to do was think of what fun thing to do next.

Suddenly, we realized we were hearing screams of terror. Someone was screaming, "My baby! My baby!" Looking out over the water toward the screams, we could see a large, empty boat, circling. Everyone had been thrown out of it. We watched in horror as the boat circled and the people in the water screamed. Finally, another boat reached them, pulling them from the bay, but not before their young son was struck in the head by the propeller.

My mother, hearing the screams, came running. She reached the dock just as the boat carrying the rescued people arrived. The rescue boat was small and, as lifeboats often are, overcrowded. Its passengers were squeezed in among those who had just pulled them to safety. It was difficult for them to climb from the boat onto the dock. They appeared dazed, uncertain of where to go or what to do next. The dock, that only moments before had been a place of laughter and fun, was now a place of panic and confusion. The mother was still screaming. The child lay unmoving, silent in his father's arms. My mother, never one to hold me, took me in her arms, shielding my eyes so that I would not see the injured child. Through all this, we could hear the sound of their empty boat, still circling.

This was the scene my father came upon when he arrived at the dock. Quickly taking charge, he led the family to our driveway where he had been washing the car. He carefully wrapped the child's head in towels from our house and helped these three strangers into the backseat of our car. As he backed out of the driveway, he yelled to my mother to call the hospital and tell them he was on his way. From our backyard we could see the bridge my father had to drive over to get to the Naval Hospital.

After he drove away, we went into the house and waited, waited for his return and the news he would bring. Hours later, he returned home. After he told us it had taken seventy-five stitches to close the young boy's wound, we all went outside to marvel that there was no blood in my father's freshly washed car.

In many ways, I experienced some of my happiest childhood memories in Pensacola's idyllic setting. Still, I possessed an underlying anger that I expressed in numerous ways.

For the first year after moving to Florida, my sister Deborah and I slept together in a double bed. Melanie still slept in a crib and David had yet to be born. My parents always believed in buying quality furniture, and they bought two solid maple bedroom sets. There were four twin beds that could be made into bunk beds, four dressers, and two bedside tables. Thinking about it now, I realize it must have been a sizable investment for a junior officer in the Navy. Well, one day I scraped the finish off my headboard with my teeth. How angry must I have been to do something like that? Where did all that anger come from? It must have come from the abuse I suffered as a baby and small child and my mother's continued verbal abuse.

In addition to or maybe because of my anger, I was also extremely jealous of my sister Deborah. Everyone loved Deborah! There was a handsome young man who lived in the neighborhood with his wife in a small apartment in my friend Mary's house. This young man liked my sister, who was about six years old, and was teaching her to fish off Uncle Joe's dock. Mary and I went to visit his wife one day, and I started a big, physical fight with Mary. The thought of it embarrassed me for years afterward.

My jealousy and anger caused great injury to my hands, and I am lucky I still have all my fingers. My father had taught Deborah how to open our overhead garage door. On this day he asked her to go out and open it. I was enraged! I was three years older! Why was I not the one opening it? I ran out behind her to the garage and grabbed the big heavy bar that moved as the door opened. Of course, I could not hold the door back with my skinny little arms, and the bar went against the wall and smashed my fingers. I was screaming, and my poor sister was jumping up and down trying to grab the door to close it but was unable to do so.

Before my father got there, I pulled my hands out, and they were a bloody mess. It was hard to see exactly what the injuries were. My father raced me over the bridge to the Naval Hospital. On the way, the fingers that were not mangled started spurting blood from the deep indentations that had been caused by the bar. Now, as I write this, my hands are disfigured by arthritis, but I am thankful that at least I have all my fingers. My mother told me that when she took me to have the bandages changed, she almost fainted when she saw my hands. This was the mother who had attended nursing school!

Chapter 3

Family Secrets

From Pensacola, we moved to Carmel Valley, California, for one year while my father attended the Naval War College in Monterey. Then in 1957 when I was starting the sixth grade, we moved back east to Virginia Beach. My parents bought a house that was surrounded by woods, farm fields, and the waters of Lynnhaven Bay. Our neighborhood was a child's paradise. It was heavily wooded, which made it pitch black at night. In those years, children were allowed to go out and play as long as we were home in time for dinner. I spent my days outside, in every season, and in all types of weather.

When I went out in the morning, my mother never knew where I went or what I was doing. I was lucky to immediately make a good friend who lived across the causeway in a large log cabin. Judy and I spent days building forts in the woods—often the boys in the neighborhood would find them and tear them down, and then we would construct another one. We used anything we could find to build them, and when they started building more houses in the neighborhood, we used scrap lumber. Along the causeway was a small beach. In the colder weather we would build a fire on the beach and roast potatoes. Somehow, we sometimes got oysters and roasted them also.

Judy's father gave us an old wooden motorboat to use. It did not have a motor. We had two oars but no oarlocks. We never wore life jackets. We may have had two in the boat, but if we did, they were probably waterlogged. One of us would sit on the bow and paddle, and the other would use the second oar as a rudder. We went all over the bay in that boat, and sometimes on windy days, I would sneak the beach umbrella out of our garage, and we would have a sailboat! When we wanted to swim in the bay, we would coat ourselves with Crisco so the jellyfish would slide off without stinging us. Often, we would see snakes swimming by. It was a Tom Sawyer and Huckleberry Finn childhood.

The family across the street from my house had a dock and let us use it to go crabbing. We tied chicken necks on strings and waited patiently for a crab to start eating. When we thought there was a crab on the line, we would slowly (and I mean SLOWLY) pull up the string. If there was a crab eating the chicken neck (and it had not gotten wise to us), the other person would scoop it up in a net. It took us hours to catch a dozen crabs. We would put them in a bushel basket, and then put that basket into the basket of my big heavy Schwinn bicycle. Sometimes the crabs would escape, and we would have to stop and chase them down the road! We could always count on Mrs. Kyle to buy them from us for fifty cents a dozen. One time we got an order from someone else for four dozen crabs. Judy and I got up very early, crabbed all day, and sold them for two dollars. One summer we decided to make as much money as we could.

In addition to crabbing, we did every odd job anyone would hire us for—including mowing someone's lawn. We put our earnings in a jar, and at the end of the summer, we each had thirteen dollars plus some change.

My bike was another freedom. In the winter Judy, her sister Harriet, my sister Deborah, and I would ride our bikes down to the ocean-front, about seven miles from our house. I was twelve and my sister was nine when we started doing this. We would spend the day riding up and down the boardwalk, and as most places were closed in the winter in those years, we would have to search for a place to have lunch. By the time we were riding home, it would be getting dark. I do not know if my mother knew where we had been. It is hard for me to imagine we did that at such a young age—but we did! I can still picture my young sister riding her little bike, pedaling furiously, trying to keep up with us on our big bikes! Unfortunately, Judy went away to a boarding school after the seventh grade, and my best friend and ally was gone except for the summers.

The school days for the sixth and seventh grades were torturous. I grew four inches during the sixth-grade school year. I was 5'4", weighed eighty-four pounds, wore a size ten shoe, had budding breasts, and a black mustache. Back then, the teacher would often leave the classroom unattended. My seventh-grade teacher was the principal's wife, and she would leave us alone for long periods of time. When the teacher was out of the room, a gang of boys and girls surrounded me chanting, "Olive Oyl, Olive Oyl," or "Leslie has a mustache. Leslie has a mustache." And I just stood there, taking their abuse, never fighting back.

After many days of arriving home crying, my mother finally suggested I remove my mustache with Nair. That did nothing but give the kids something else to chant. Now, they chanted "Leslie shaves. Leslie shaves." They would chant it when I got on the bus even when I was in the eighth and ninth grades.

I did have a lovely sixth-grade teacher, Miss Welch, who said to me one day on the playground, "Leslie, I wish I would be able to see you when you are sixteen because you are going to be very beautiful." The one bright spot in my life! Unfortunately, she left in the middle of the year to get married, and she was replaced by a man who paddled the last person to return from the restroom—of course there always has to be a last person!

Recently, I came across some pictures of myself as a young woman. I was shocked to see myself. I was not beautiful. I was gorgeous, and I never knew it. I think I always felt like that Ugly Duckling, Olive Oyl with big feet and a black mustache.

My mother did nothing to help me overcome this image. In fact, she did everything to reinforce it. She constantly told me that my one sister was the most beautiful of the three of us and the other was the most intelligent. Where did that leave me? What was I? Surprisingly, one day when I was a teenager, I said something about my being pretty, and she said, "Oh, you are not that pretty." My mother actually had three beautiful daughters, but she could not enjoy that fact. I think she was so fragile that even though she was a very beautiful woman, she was jealous of our beauty.

My mother did all she could do to make sure the four of us children were not close to each other. She was something like the mother in *Prince of Tides*, who told each of her children that he/she was her favorite. My mother did it the opposite way—at least to me—by telling me my younger sister was her favorite and the only one whose birth was planned. The other three of us were apparently accidents. I certainly know I was because I was born nine months and nine days after my parents married, and my mother constantly let me know that I had been a problem from the day I was born.

Whenever my mother told me what she thought of me, I said nothing in return. I intuitively knew it would be lethal to do so. I believed what she said about me was true. How could I not? She was my mother. Also, the abuse I suffered as a baby had silenced me. How else could one explain that as a toddler I would sit on an ottoman, alone in a room and not move until my mother came back and told me I could move? When I was in my forties and rooming in a woman's house, one of her friends told me I was like a ghost. No one knew I was there. From the time I was a small baby I had received the message that I was not wanted, and I did my best to disappear.

I often wondered what caused my mother to act the way she did. It wasn't until I was in my early sixties that I learned why my mother was such a troubled person. I was sitting on my couch in Maine and my sister Deborah called to tell me about her visit with our parents. She and her partner, Linda, had spent Thanksgiving with them. Deborah was telling me that my mother had become furious with Linda when she had taken my mother's laundry out of the dryer to fold it. My mother had yelled at Linda to never touch her laundry. Deborah asked me, "Why would Mother do that? Why would she be so mean to Linda about the laundry?"

I, who at this time had been estranged from my parents for almost twenty years, said, "Deborah, you are always trying to make sense of a crazy family. You cannot make sense out of craziness."

Deborah replied, "Well, what about this? Uncle Alfred was Mother's father." I immediately started crying.

"You mean Uncle Alfred was our grandfather and we never knew it?" I sobbed.

When we were growing up, a man named Tom Brown, who we knew as Grandpa, came to see us once every four or five years. Grandpa was an extremely homely man. He was 6'2" and was skin and bones. My mother always said he weighed 130 pounds, but even as thin as he was, that is hard to believe. He was very dark-skinned and had a large nose and large ears. I have always said he looked like Gandhi, but, actually, that is doing Gandhi an injustice. He chain-smoked unfiltered Camel cigarettes, lighting one from another. He was aloof, an imposing presence. He stood and sat ram-rod straight. He was not a warm person. I cannot remember ever having a conversation with him. Every time he came my mother was a nervous wreck.

When we were children, our other visitor, Alfred (who we called *Uncle*), came and spent two weeks with us at Christmas and two weeks with us during the summer. At this time, he was working as the Head of the Laundry Department at the Federal Prison in Milan, Michigan. Those four weeks must have been most, if not all, of his vacation time. Uncle Alfred was a mystery to us children. We would ask our mother how he was related to us. Who was Uncle Alfred? She would tell us he had been a friend of her mother's, and that was all the information she ever gave us. When he was elderly and had dementia, he lived with my parents. I would say to my mother that I thought he was too much for her to care for. She would answer that she had promised her mother she would always take care of him. And I would think—*that does not make sense. My grandmother died when my mother was thirteen. Who asks a thirteen-year-old child to take care of an adult?*

Uncle Alfred was a handsome, elegant man. He would drive up in his beautifully polished, black 1940s-era Plymouth and step out immaculately dressed. In the winter, he wore a gray wool overcoat, a gray dress hat, and leather gloves. Uncle smoked two cigarettes a day, which he smoked in a sleek cigarette holder. He carried a little notebook in his pocket and made shorthand notes in it throughout the day. He had been a stenographer in the Navy during World War I. What he did with those notes, we never knew. When he wrote something in his beautiful penmanship, he used purple ink. Uncle played the violin in a symphony orchestra and would bring his violin and his beautifully carved wooden music stand with him. I can remember him standing in our small living room practicing his music.

Uncle was a quiet man, and I am sure being around four boisterous children in a small house was an adjustment for him every time he came. Although, working in a prison that is filled with loud noises may have made being with us a quiet retreat. He expressed his discomfort by going around muttering to himself, "Oh, my! Oh, my!" Or he would make a *tsk tsk* sound with his tongue. When I was about six years old, he was sitting next to me at the breakfast table. I spilled my orange juice all over him. He jumped up exclaiming, "Oh, my! Oh, my!"

When he returned after changing his clothes, I spilled my milk all over him. Poor Uncle! I doubt he ever sat next to me again. Then one time when I was in my teens, he surprised me when I ran down the hall in the nude from the bathroom to my bedroom. My mother admonished me about the incident by telling me Uncle said to her, "Oh, my, Adalynne, Leslie is getting to be a big girl, isn't she?" I guess I had surprised him more than he had surprised me!

The only time we ever went out to dinner when we were children was when Uncle came. He would treat all of us to dinner in a lovely restaurant at least once if not twice when he was there. He paid for our schooling, and I am sure he gave my parents the down payment when they bought their house in Virginia in 1957. Alfred was German, and at Christmas, my mother always had two of his favorite things for him—stollen and marzipan. Although she always paid attention to his needs, she was often very nasty to him. Of course, she was that way with the rest of her family, too.

This is the story my mother told my sister and Linda the night before they left from their Thanksgiving visit. My grandmother Bessie was married to Tom Brown, Grandpa. My grandmother and Tom Brown had three children who survived and lived to adulthood—Uncle Tommy, Uncle Billy, and Aunt Annette. Annette, the youngest of the three, was five years older than my mother. Uncle Alfred was a boarder in their home, which was not an uncommon thing in those years. My grandmother became pregnant by Alfred, and my mother was born in 1924. They lived on Long Island, and when my mother was two years old, she, my grandmother, and Alfred took the train to California. They were going to try to start a life without Tom Brown. For some reason, it did not work out, and my grandmother got in touch with Tom Brown, her husband, and asked him to send her three tickets so they could return to live with him on Long Island.

My mother said to my sister and Linda, "Why did she ask for three tickets? Why didn't she leave Alfred in California?"

Upon their return, my grandmother became pregnant by Alfred with my Uncle Robert. Robert died of scarlet fever when he was four or five years old. My mother said the children at school called her a bastard, and people seeing my grandmother and my mother walking down the street, would cross to the other side.

My mother had to call Tom Brown "Daddy" when she was at home, but when she went out with Alfred and my grandmother, she had to call Alfred "Daddy." When my grandmother died, Alfred left my mother to be raised by Tom Brown. My sister asked my mother why Alfred did not take her with him, and she told my sister that Alfred could never have taken care of her.

After hearing my sister tell this story, I said to her, "No wonder mother did not want Linda to touch her laundry—she had aired what she always thought of as her dirty laundry the night before." Apparently, everyone else in the family knew the story except my mother's four children.

I asked Deborah and Linda who were on speaker phone why my mother had told them this, and Linda answered, "Your mother said it was because she had been watching Dr. Phil!"

We had so many questions, but the next time my sister and Linda went to visit, my father told my sister not to talk about Alfred—it was too upsetting to my mother. So, we never were able to find out any more of the story.

But, using the things my mother told me as I was growing up, I imagine this is what happened when my grandmother died.

My grandmother died when my mother was thirteen. The morning after the funeral, as she started down the stairs, she stopped. Her father's bags were packed and sitting by the front door. A sob caught in her throat. Was he leaving? Was he planning on going without saying goodbye?

Listening, she heard Tom, her mother's husband, and Alfred, her mother's lover and her father, arguing. Tom's voice was raised, "She isn't my child." Alfred said something, but she could hear only part of it.

Tom was louder: "Now that Bess is gone, you have no right to leave her here with me."

Gone, her mother was gone. She had spent the last two years watching her mother die. Just as her own breasts were beginning to bud, her mother's had been removed, cut off, discarded. Her mother's death had been a slow, painful death. Tom, forever angry, had said it was just what she deserved. Alfred, always tender toward her mother, had tried to make her comfortable, but there was nothing he could do.

She had walked in on her mother bathing one day shortly before she died. Her mother's once lovely body was emaciated, ugly red scars slashed across her chest. She gasped then, and her mother started to cry, "Oh, Adalynne, I never wanted you to see." Was that the day her mother made her promise she would always take care of Alfred? Now that he was leaving, how could she keep the promise?

She heard Tom again. "God only knows why I tolerated you all these years, living under my roof, sleeping with my wife."

She could hear Alfred this time when he said, "You know why, Tom."

But she didn't know why. She knew her mother kept her home from school because of the taunting. She knew people crossed to the other side of the street to avoid her and her mother, but that was all she knew. The rest she didn't understand. She didn't understand why Tom was to be called "Daddy" when she was home with him.

And why Alfred was to be called "Daddy" when she and her mother were out with him.

Her mother was gone. Just the day before, she had watched her mother's casket slowly roll on a conveyor belt into the mortician's furnace. Alfred had refused to attend, calling it ghoulish, a morbid way to celebrate a life. But Tom had insisted she go, making her take a front row seat. She had wanted to cry, but Tom had forbidden her to cry, saying, "You are not to shed tears over your mother's death."

She tried to block out the image of her mother's coffin going by on the other side of the glass. She concentrated on the organ music, but the record was scratched. It kept skipping, then getting stuck, playing the same note over and over and over again. It was so hot; she could hardly breathe. The sweat was running down her chest and soaking her dress. If only she could faint as her mother would have done, timing it to interrupt any unpleasant thing she did not want to deal with.

Alfred came rushing into the entryway and saw her standing there. All he said was, "Oh Adalynne." Taking his bags he left, leaving her behind.

When my grandmother died, and Alfred left, Tom Brown raised my mother. My mother's half siblings had all left home by this time. Tom Brown fired their full-time housekeeper and cook, and her responsibilities became my mother's. My mother had to be home from school and have dinner on the table when Tom Brown arrived home from work, and everything had to be perfect with the rolls hot and just the right shade of brown. No wonder my mother was a wreck when Tom Brown came to visit us.

Although my mother stated emphatically that Tom Brown was her father because he raised her, he rarely visited us. On the other hand, every year, Alfred spent two weeks with us at Christmas and two weeks with us in the summer. All those years and the secret was kept. My sisters, my brother, and I were the only ones in the family who did not know. We children were told Uncle Alfred was just a friend of our grandmother's. I know we would have had a different relationship with him if we had known he was our grandfather. We rarely saw any of our other relatives. He was the only one we saw regularly, and we did not know who he was.

The few times I have told this story to anyone, they have said it must have been money. But I know it was not money. Tom Brown had a good job with AT&T all through the Depression. If it was not money, it was sex. I think Tom Brown and Alfred were lovers, and Alfred also had sex with my grandmother. Why else would Tom Brown allow another man to live in his home and impregnate his wife? Recently, my sister and I came across a picture of Tom Brown and Alfred standing close together. My sister turned to me and said, "Have you ever seen two men gayer than that?"

This secret explained so much to me about my mother, and when I learned it, I was able to finally, fully forgive her. Because she was never able to realize it had nothing to do with her, my mother's shame crippled her and made it impossible for her to love or feel she was lovable. I am sad that she was never able in this lifetime to overcome it and experience the freedom that would have come with doing so. Had she been able to release her past, it could have changed everything. Her shame impacted the lives of her four children. We have all had psychological problems and problems with addiction, and we have passed those things on to our children, quietly and shamefully.

Chapter 4

A Not-So-Chosen Path

After my ninth-grade year, we moved every summer. I escaped my bullies, but the price I had to pay was that I had to constantly adjust to a new school and make new friends. My senior year we lived in Guantanamo Bay, Cuba. My father was the commanding officer of the one squadron that was stationed there. Because he was one of the commanding officers on the base, we had a lovely home at the end of a street. We were high above the water and could see all the ships coming and going, seaplanes landing, and the sailboats from the sailing club.

The base got all its water from Cuba, and we were there the year Castro decided he was going to charge more for it. I don't know how high up the command the decision was made, but the Admiral of the base went out and cut the water pipe, and we basically had no water. There was some in the storage tanks. So, until the first tankers arrived with water, we had water three hours a day—one hour at each mealtime. What a crimp that made in my social life— my main entertainment had been to go to the pool and meet the young officers who were off the ships that were there for training. However, the pools were closed for about six months while a water desalination plant was built, so I started going to the beach instead. There was a bluff above the beach where Cuban military men stood guard looking down at us Americans frolicking in the sun in beautiful clear Caribbean water. I spent much of my time on a large swing, swinging by the hour clad only in my bikini.

This is something I wrote during my senior year in Guantanamo Bay. Like many things I have written, it came to me fully written. It does give a picture of how I had been feeling ever since I was a young child.

Alone

The day dawned heavily.

And the mist strangled the Sun.

And I wanted to scream
to let the World know I
acknowledged the wound She had
inflicted upon my heart.

Scream!

I wanted to scream or run.

I had to release something.

Something that was hidden deep within me.

The emotion had no name.

But its strength was destroying me
and leaving me an empty shell.

Scream!

I must scream.

The Hill on which I stood was solid.

And I screamed.

And the Earth echoed my scream
magnified a thousand times
for She could not stand the knowledge
of Her crime.

I threw myself upon the Earth.

And I screamed.

And the Sky began to weep softly.

And I screamed
until I could scream no more.

And I lay there sobbing.

Alone

Alone

I had always had an intense desire to learn and wanted very much to go to college. Even though I moved every year I was in high school, I took the hardest classes to prepare me to do so. However, for as long as I could remember, my mother told me I should be a secretary. Because my mother had such a strong influence on me, instead of college, I went from what I thought of as a prison—Guantanamo Bay—to the wonders of New York City where I attended Katharine Gibbs Secretarial School. I went from a small base on a small island with only forty-three seniors in my class to one of the largest cities in the world. The only secretarial class I had taken in high school was typing in my senior year, and I took that only because the high school did not offer many classes that I had not already taken.

At Katharine Gibbs, those of us who had not had any secretarial training were put in classes with those girls who had taken secretarial classes all through high school. Starting out, they could take shorthand and type faster than I could ever dream of doing. I never did get the hang of shorthand, and consequently, every letter I wrote was stamped in big letters—UNMAILABLE!! Never once did I produce a mailable letter!

Most of the girls were commuters, but those of us who were not lived in the Barbizon Hotel for Women on East 63rd Street and Lexington Avenue. It was jokingly called The Vertical Nunnery. There were always men sitting in the lobby hoping to meet one of the young women who lived there. There were a number of floors designated as Katharine Gibbs floors. Men were not allowed above the mezzanine floor, and in those days, it was strictly enforced. If there was a repairman on the floor, we heard someone calling, "Man on the floor! Man on the floor!"

I had one of the best rooms on the fourteenth floor. It was a corner room with windows on each wall. We had a sink in the room, and the toilets and showers were communal and right outside my door. We were served breakfast and dinner five days a week in the dining room for the Katharine Gibbs students. We had to buy our lunches and all our meals on the weekends. This caused us to find some of the wonderful little restaurants on Third Avenue. I made some lovely friends. Mimi was four years older than I, and she would lovingly say, "I invited Leslie to come visit one night, and she never left!" My friends slept in on the weekends. Since I was an early riser, I would get up and explore the city for a couple of hours before returning to the hotel and having breakfast with the late risers.

We rode the bus in the morning to Katharine Gibbs and the subway back to the hotel in the afternoon—something my mother warned me never to do. I wore a gold suede coat in the winter, and because we were packed into both the bus in the morning and the subway in the afternoon, I noticed many men get off with their dark suits covered in gold suede! Katharine Gibbs was located in what at the time was named the Pan-Am Building, which was located at 200 Park Avenue. We had to wear hats and gloves and, of course, heels and stockings. Our hair could not touch our shoulders, and we were not allowed to wear sweaters. People would stop and stare when the elevators opened in the afternoon and hundreds of young women in hats and gloves would disembark.

As part of our training, we had to call actual businesses and set up mock job interviews. I still remember the man with whom I had an interview. I remember him because during the entire interview, he never once looked at me. He sat and read his mail as if I were not even in the room. One afternoon my friend Mimi was having one of her interviews. I offered to take her books back to the hotel so that she would not have to take them with her. She carried her books in a briefcase. I carried mine in a satchel in my arms. When I got to the subway, I put my token in, and not being accustomed to a brief-case, I pushed the turnstile bar with it. The next bar came up and got caught between my legs! There I was sitting atop that bar in my hat and gloves with both hands weighted down with books! As I sat up there with that cold bar between my legs, people streamed by on either side of me as if a young woman in a hat and gloves sitting on the turnstile bar was an everyday occurrence! I have always imag-ined that I was a funny story told around many dinner tables that night. Our friend Kathy was with me and had gone ahead of me.

I called to her, "KATHY!" Kathy was very nearsighted and vain—not a good combination, for she refused to wear her glasses even though she could see very little without them. We had to lead her all over the city!

When I called to her, she came right up to me, squinted her eyes and said, "What are you doing up there!?!"

I said, "Forget what I am doing here and take these books so I can get off!" I got off on the wrong side and had to buy another fifteen-cent token.

Because the Katharine Gibbs course was for one school year only, I went home in May of 1965 with my stack of UNMAILABLE letters. I was returning home having failed to become what my mother had always told me I should be. That being the only guidance I ever received from either parent, I had no sense of what I could do or be. My year in New York had been exciting. There was no reason why I could not have stayed and found roommates and a job, but because I had no self-confidence or feelings of self-worth, I did not. I drifted through my life never planning or thinking of what I might do.

My family was living in Virginia Beach, Virginia, where we had lived before moving to Guantanamo Bay. I was taking the summer off with the idea I would look for a job in the fall—although I had no idea what I was qualified to do. That summer my brother was nine years old, and one of his friends had a crush on me. My brother, David, would regularly deliver love notes from my nine-year-old admirer. At the bottom of one of the notes it said, "If you answer, please print."

I kept that sweet note for years, but don't know what happened to it. My brother told me years later that Scott had been paying him to be the mailman. Now as I look back, I imagine there were men who secretly admired me. But I was not a warm and approachable woman, and consequently, they did not let their feelings be known. I once read an essay on the paradox of the beautiful woman. People think beautiful women have much attention from men. But most men are afraid to approach a beautiful woman and, therefore, she is often alone and lonely. My mother would tell me about all the men who had been in love with her, and she would end by saying, "But you would not know about that. You have not had many men care about you." My mother did her best to ensure that that was true.

My father was the air boss on the *USS America*, a brand-new aircraft carrier. That summer of 1965 on July 6th, the ship had a Dependents' Day Cruise. The people stationed on the ship (in those days, it was only men) could bring their families aboard for the day. The ship would go out to sea and catapult jets off of its flight deck to show the family members what was done when the ship was out. We had embarked on the ship from the pier in the morning, but when the day was over, the ship anchored out. That meant that all of us had to be taken back to the pier in launches.

As we waited for our turn to be taken ashore, my family sat in the lounge of the wardroom where the officers of the ship ate. As we sat and waited, a friend of my father's brought a young officer over to meet me. He was one of the dental officers on the ship. He had seen me in December when I was out with my parents at one of the Navy clubs. That day he had seen me come aboard in the morning. His date for the day missed the cruise because she was in court about a traffic ticket—one of those fateful things that changes the whole direction of one's life. If she had been there, Jerry and I would not have married four months later.

Yes, it was a whirlwind courtship. In those four months, Jerry wined and dined me and took me to meet his family in Tennessee. He told me later that the night we met he looked up my father's records to see if we were Catholic. His last love had been a Catholic, and his Baptist parents were very against their relationship because of it. But even though I was not Catholic—I was a Presbyterian—his mother never did like me. I am sure no woman would have ever been good enough for her son. Jerry had two brothers, and I do not think Myrna cared for their wives either.

Most women get excited about the prospect of a wedding and the life that comes afterward, but looking back, I realize I went through life without thinking or planning. I just did things with no plans. I think I walked through life zombie-like—a very unhappy, depressed, angry zombie. I had learned to do what I called going away or dis-associating or detaching as a young child. It had protected me then, and it had become so automatic for me that I did it without realizing I was doing it. On the phone one night, Jerry said he would be moving to Tennessee to start private practice when he got out of the Navy in a couple of months.

I said, "Well, don't expect me to sit around here waiting for you."

He replied, "Then, let's get married."

On that romantic note, I said, "Okay."

Jerry was getting out of the Navy before the ship was leaving in early December for a six-month Mediterranean cruise. We had to get married before it left so my father would be there for the wedding. I had met Jerry in July and was planning our wedding in October. While I was planning the wedding, Jerry was at sea. My father had gotten emergency leave and had gone to New York with my mother because his father had just died. I remember I did the planning, what little there was, by myself. The first time I met with the minister, whom I did not know, I was alone, and he treated me with cool indifference. The second time Jerry and I went together, and the minister talked to Jerry, ignoring my presence.

Jerry got out of the Navy one day, and we got married the next—November 27, 1965. I was nineteen, he was ten years older. I had wanted a small wedding, but my father and Jerry thought we had to invite all the officers from the ship. I do not remember how many people attended, but I do know the large church was full, and as I walked down the aisle and looked at the faces, there were very few people I recognized. Two of my friends from Katharine Gibbs came, one from Atlanta, and one from Florida. They must have stayed in our house, but I cannot imagine where they slept as we had a very small house. Weddings then were not the elaborate affairs they are today and mine, though very nice, was particularly spartan.

I Am the Whisper of the Wind

My mother and father had the rehearsal dinner at our house. Jerry's mother just sat in a chair, wringing her hands, and looking as if she were attending a funeral, not a wedding. We had the reception at the Oceana Naval Air Station Officers' Club, which was the one closest to the church but certainly not the nicest one in the area. The room was not decorated for the reception. There was no head table, and no toasts were made. There was no dancing as there was no music. There were just a lot of people drinking.

My sister Deborah, who was sixteen at the time, was my only attendant. I did my own hair and makeup, got into my dress at home, and my father drove me to the church. My dress had been made by a dressmaker my mother had used for years. It was a simple, elegant dress made from a Vogue pattern. There had been a wedding in the church earlier in the day, and we shared the flowers and split the expense.

A couple of hours before the wedding, my nine-year-old brother fell out of his tree house and broke his arm. My father took him to the nearest Navy clinic and called me to say he would not be able to give me away. He had to take my brother to the Naval Hospital in Portsmouth to have his arm set. When I got off the phone and told my friends from Katherine Gibbs, we all cried. At the last minute, another one of the naval officers offered to take my brother to the hospital so that my father wouldn't miss the wedding. When my brother arrived at the reception with his arm in a cast, he was the star of the show. The bride was forgotten—she was just the reason for a good Navy party!

Jerry and I went to NYC for our honeymoon, staying in a horrible Howard Johnsons with 40-watt light bulbs and stains on the carpet. I remember the name of one of the two shows we went to: *The Roar of the Grease Paint - The Smell of the Crowd.*

One very interesting thing happened. We went up to the top of the Empire State Building (Don't all honeymooners do that?). It was just before closing, and there was one other couple there. Jerry walked around the pillar and put out his hand to shake the hand of someone he had gone to Dental School with.

I started crying on our honeymoon and continued to cry for the next twenty-four years—hence the poem on my dedication page, which is actually something Jerry said to me. Jerry and I went to a few sessions of marriage counseling after we had been married fifteen years.

The counselors were a couple, and when Jerry asked, "How long is she going to cry?"

The husband answered, "Until she is finished."

I did not know why I was crying. I had been an unhappy child, and for some reason my depression became worse when I married.

When I was in my forties and had left Jerry, I did begin to stop crying with the help of a wonderful psychiatrist. He helped me uncover the deep wounds I had suffered as a baby and young child. I had been abused by my mother and sexually abused by my father's father, with whom we lived for the first year of my life. I always had a strange knowing that I'd suffered great horror at my grandfather's hands, but it took a very skilled psychiatrist to help me uncover these preverbal memories which came to me in dreams and visions in that state between wakefulness and sleep.

I believe these memories to be true because after having them and being helped by Dr. P to feel the horror of them, I began to heal, and my deep, lifelong depression began to dissipate. As my depression dissipated, my tears subsided. The hurtful, demoralizing things my mother had said to me were the things I had been playing over and over in my mind. I believe I had to remember the preverbal abuse before I could begin to erase those tapes.

Chapter 5

Married Life

When we got back to my parents' home in Virginia, we loaded up a tiny U-Haul trailer with the only possessions we owned in the world—all our wedding gifts—silver trays, silver bowls, silver candy dishes, and silver bud vases. There were so many things we needed, and all we had were silver things that tarnished until they turned black. Each time we moved, we never unpacked that box. We just moved it from place to place.

I am sure there were many brides who would have loved getting all that silver, but I certainly wasn't one of them. I never was or have been a formal person. I am most comfortable in jeans and an old shirt. The only thing I brought to the marriage was a wooden clothes rack that I had antiqued. We were moving to Murfreesboro, Tennessee, where Jerry had gone to college and where one of his sisters lived with her family. Murfreesboro is about thirty miles from Lebanon, where he grew up and where his mother and father and grandmother still lived in the house he had grown up in.

We arrived in Tennessee with no useful possessions and no money, but we were prepared to put on a fancy party! We had the silver serving dishes but no money to buy any food to go into them. Jerry had a job waiting for him. He had arranged to practice dentistry in the office of one of the older dentists in town. The dentist had told him he would refer so many patients to him that Jerry would never have to worry about running out of business, but in the two and a half years Jerry practiced there, the older dentist did not refer one single patient. Jerry always said he thought the man was unhappy that Jerry arrived in town with a wife since the older dentist had a daughter of marrying age. Who knows why people do things or don't do things?

There I was a very young bride in a foreign land, learning how to be a wife. Jerry often came home and told me how he had run into an old girlfriend of his. Instead of telling me how much I meant to him, Jerry spent two whole evenings telling me in detail about all the women he had slept with. Why did I listen? It wasn't so different from my mother telling me that I was not important. I was accustomed to being talked to in that way.

This was my first and only experience of living in the Bible Belt. Because Jerry was the new dentist in town, every minister came, one at a time, to encourage us to attend his church. One minister told Jerry, while I sat by his side, that if he came to his church, he could see his old girlfriend in the choir every Sunday. Was I that good at being invisible?

It was a strange experience for me. I had traveled all over the country, lived in seven different places, and I was now living among people who had never left the place where they had been born. However, even though I often had to spell the word I was saying (I had been raised by two Yankees), everyone was very warm and welcoming—except, of course, my mother-in-law. Unfortunately, Jerry repeated every single nasty thing she said to him about me. It was not until this very moment as I am writing this that I realize that was part of his abuse.

Jerry was opening a dental office in January, the worst month of the year to start a practice or to be in practice—who wants to spend money on their teeth right after Christmas? Because neither one of us had any money, we borrowed the money Jerry needed to equip the office along with a little extra to live on until he started seeing patients. Jerry had a friend who owned several apartment complexes, and we rented a furnished apartment from him. Jerry would come home for lunch, and I would often go back to the office with him for the afternoon. Even though I never produced a mailable letter, I had learned a few things at Katharine Gibbs and was able to take care of the paperwork involved with the practice. The apartment we were renting was small and cheaply furnished. Every evening during dinner, Jerry would look around and say, "I hate this carpet. When I carpet my office, I want something very different."

Little did we know as we sat there each evening looking at the carpet that it would soon become the central role in a story that would become part of our marital lore. Jerry called to tell me he was on his way home for lunch. The conversation went something like this:

"Leslie, I'm ready to come home for lunch. Are you coming back with me to work on the books?"

"Yes, but ...."

"What's wrong?"

"Well, I have done something that is going to ruin your whole day—no, your whole week."

"You have? What is it?"

I looked down at the carpet. "I'll tell you when you get home."

"No, tell me now."

"Uh, you know how small the kitchen is."

"Yes. What has that got to do with it?"

"Well, I was baking cookies, chocolate cookies. You remember the ones we had at your sister's? The ones you liked so much."

"What did you do?"

"Well, I forgot I had stored the iron skillet in the oven. When I went to put the cookies in to bake, I didn't know where to put it. The kitchen was a wreck. I put it on the carpet."

"So?"

I took a deep breath. "It melted the carpet down to the backing."

"Okay, I'll look at it when I get home."

"Look at it! It's the first thing you will see when you walk in the door!"

And now we were looking down at a melted circle in that carpet he hated.

"My God, Leslie! What have you done?"

Printed in mirror image were the words *13" iron skillet.* I did not start crying until Jerry, thinking we would have to replace the carpet, said, "Maybe they can cut this carpet down and put it in my office."

Jerry's worries and my tears were for naught because the maintenance man for the apartment complex cut the damaged piece out and replaced it. It wasn't long before we were laughing at my blunder.

A couple of weeks later, a woman from the Welcome Wagon knocked on our door. She handed me a basket of goodies and invited me to their monthly luncheon. On the day of the luncheon, she picked me up and then drove two doors down to pick up Roberta, another newcomer. When Roberta got into the car, I knew instantly that we would be friends. Although ten years older than I, Roberta was also a newlywed.

I started to tell the two women my story about the carpet, and Roberta excitedly interrupted me with, "You didn't burn your carpet too, did you?"

When I told her I had, she said, "When Bill came home and saw what I had done, he said 'Only a stupid idiot would do something like that!' I can't wait to tell him there is another stupid idiot, and she lives just two doors down!" Bill and Roberta and Jerry and I did become good friends and had many laughs over Roberta's many crazy mishaps.

A few months went by, and Jerry was finally having his office carpet installed. The man laying the carpet asked Jerry if he wanted him to keep the leftover pieces of carpet. When Jerry said that sounded like a good idea, the man said, "Yes, you never know what might happen. Two dumb broads over at the Deville Apartments both burned their carpet."

Jerry looked at the man and said, "I'll have you know one of those dumb broads is my wife!"

Soon after the carpet debacle, we moved to a nicer, unfurnished apartment with a swimming pool right outside our door. After we had been married for six months, Roberta was pregnant and so was another friend. When Jerry got home from work one day, I said, "All my friends are pregnant. I want to get pregnant too."

It did not take long for that to happen, and our first child, a daughter we named Kelly, was born the day after Valentine's Day 1967. I was twenty years old. Our second child, a son, was born in March of 1970.

On the outside, I was doing all the things a young wife and mother does, but on the inside, I was still the miserably depressed person I had been since childhood. I cried constantly. My depression and Jerry's anger created a very tumultuous relationship. And since history repeats itself, we passed on the traumas of our childhoods. Our children were caught in the crossfire of our violent arguments and physical fights.

After being in private practice for a little over two years, Jerry decided he wanted to go back into the Navy. He said that when he had been in the Navy, he had seen the bright lights. But when he looked around the small town we lived in, he imagined going to the same country club parties with the same people, playing golf with the same foursome year after year, and then one day being buried in the cemetery outside of town. It was a dreadful thought.

I was excited by the thought of moving and experiencing new things and meeting new people. Jerry's parents were horrified by the idea. His father, a Tennessean, said, "I served in France in WWI and worked in the oil fields of Texas for a couple of years, and I can tell you that the only good people in the world live in Tennessee." I wondered at the time what that said about me. I definitely was not from Tennessee. I had lived all over the country—and had been raised by two Yankees!

Jerry's grandmother died about two months after Jerry left his private practice, and we had moved from Tennessee to Jerry's first duty station in Coronado, California. It was 1968, and Kelly was one year old.

When Jerry returned home for the funeral, his mother told him his grandmother had never been the same after he moved away, implying that it was his leaving that caused his grandmother to die. The interesting thing is that we would not have gone to visit his parents if it had not been for me. I was the one who told Jerry he needed to see his parents; otherwise, we would not have gone. We did not go often, and it was never an easy visit when we went.

One year when Jerry was getting ready to go on an eight-month cruise aboard the *USS Enterprise,* we visited his parents before he left. I was taking antidepressants and had a bad reaction to the medication and was sick in bed. His aunts and uncles came to see him, and even though I ended up having to go to the emergency room, his mother told him that my staying in bed and not getting up to visit with his aunts and uncles was the rudest thing she had ever seen. I cannot think of one thing she liked about me, but I also cannot think of any reason why Jerry repeated her hateful comments except to hurt me.

As we were being packed up to move to California, we gave Kelly Oreo cookies to keep her happy and out of the way, and she had black diarrhea halfway across the country! We rented a small house on Coronado which was within walking distance of the village. This was before the bridge was built, and the only way to get to San Diego was by ferry or to drive across the causeway.

Coronado was a sleepy little town with lovely shops. Every afternoon Kelly and I walked into town and explored. There were flowers everywhere, and the weather was glorious. The days were sunny, and the air was fresh with that wonderful velvety feeling. I thought I had arrived in paradise! I had not realized how much it had adversely affected me to have Jerry's family and his old friends and old girlfriends surrounding me. In California, I felt free. The friends we made were not connected to Jerry and his past. There were alleyways behind the houses and our garage was off the alleyway. Our washer and dryer were in the garage, which meant I had to cross the backyard to do the wash.

One morning I went to put some laundry into the washer, and Kelly closed the back door, locking me out. The door was glass, so Kelly stood at the door looking out at me and calling me "Lellie," which is what she called me for the first two years of her life. I was in my nightgown and bathrobe. Because our chairs had cane seats, they had worn a hole in the seat of my quilted bathrobe and the batting was hanging out! One of the windows was open, so I knew if someone would boost me up, I could get into the house. Kelly was too young to understand when I asked her to open the door. I am not sure she was physically capable of doing it anyway. I had not met the neighbors, but I needed help and fast. When my next-door neighbor answered her door, I introduced myself and told her what my problem was.

She immediately said, "My husband is in the shower. We'll have to wait a few minutes until he is out."

I said "Oh, no! I cannot have him boost me up—I do not have any underpants on!"

The woman definitely agreed with me and was able to help me climb through the window. I knew from then on to be sure the door was unlocked when I went out to the garage.

After only six months in Coronado—just after I had gotten all the grout cleaned between the tile on the kitchen counters and had gotten all the many shutters cleaned, Jerry got orders to Okinawa. It was during the Vietnam War, and he was to be stationed with the Marines. The Marines do not have their own medical or dental officers, so the Navy provides those services. It was an unaccompanied tour. The day the packers and movers came was the day Jerry was given a farewell party at work, which left me alone to take care of Kelly and work with the packers.

Packers are like locusts. They come swarming in and pack everything in sight—they have even been known to pack people's garbage! I had all the papers I would need, plus my license and Navy ID card in my purse. I knew they would pack it if I put it down. So, I carried it around all day until they had finished packing. Then thinking it was safe to do so, I put it up in a high cabinet in an empty room. Just as the movers were driving away, I went to the cabinet to get my bag, and it was not there! It had been packed and was now on a truck on its way to Virginia.

Jerry started complaining about how hard the day had been. And I said, "Wait a minute! You were not even here. You were out being feted, drinking and eating." I did have the good sense to not give Kelly Oreos this time.

Jerry drove Kelly and me back to Virginia Beach, so I could be near my family. Kelly and I lived in an apartment about ten minutes from my parents and sisters and brother who were still living at home. I was extremely close to my parents, especially my mother. How could that be when she had been and was still so verbally abusive to me? I did not recognize her treatment of me as abuse. I knew the things she said were extremely hurtful, but it is what I was accustomed to. Of course, my mother was good to me at times, but I never knew when she would lash out with one of her nasty comments. And at this time, I had yet to remember the abuse I had suffered at her hands as a baby and small child. When someone is as unaware as I was, they are often very close to their abuser because they are hoping to be loved by that person who is unable to truly love them. This certainly was true for me.

Our apartment was very sparsely furnished. All of our furniture was in storage, and I bought just a few things to make the apartment comfortable. I spent much time sewing clothes for Kelly and me and have no memory of what Kelly was doing while I sewed. She was two years old that year, so she was too young to go out and play on her own. We spent a lot of time at my parents' house, most nights having cocktails with them and their neighbors.

My childhood friend Judy came and lived with us for a couple of months. I cannot remember what her situation was, but it was fun having her there. She talked me into going with her to a woman who did electrolysis to remove the hair from our upper lips. Every time I had a treatment, my lip would swell grotesquely. It would be so swollen, it would turn inside out. After many extremely painful sessions and weeks of having to stay home so that I would not frighten little children, I stopped going. And after all that, I do not think it got rid of one hair! So, to get rid of my mustache, I would buy a block of wax, heat it in a tin can, put the hot wax on with a wooden tongue depressor, and rip it off after it had hardened.

Kelly and I were able to visit Jerry for two months during his tour. The trip from Virginia Beach to Okinawa went like this—Kelly and I were driven to the airport in Norfolk. From Norfolk we flew to what was then Washington National Airport (which now is Ronald

Reagan Washington National Airport). We took a bus to Dulles Airport and then flew cross-country, stopping and changing planes in at least two places before reaching Seattle where we had a six-hour layover. Then we had a nine-hour flight to Japan. When we arrived in Japan, we boarded a bus and drove one hour to a hotel where we spent six hours. I had been unable to sleep on the flight, but Kelly had had no problem sleeping. So, when we arrived at the hotel in Japan, she was wide awake. I could not keep my eyes open, so I slept, and I have no idea what she did during that time. Then the next morning we got back on the bus to go to the airport to get on a plane to Okinawa. Thankfully, that flight was less than two hours.

Arriving in Okinawa, we were greeted by a beaming husband and father. We got into Jerry's car for another two-hour leg of the journey. The cars on Okinawa were recycled (as one man left to go home, he sold his car to his replacement). Jerry had a very old Renault. When he drove around a corner, the back doors flew open. To solve that problem, he tied a rope from one door to the other. And we let our precious child sit back there with no seat belt. This had been a grueling journey, chasing a two-year-old around airports, sitting hours on planes that in those days did not have movies to keep your mind occupied so you would forget for a moment how extremely uncomfortable you were. To put it mildly—I was completely spent! The last thing I wanted to hear was that Jerry had bought a two-burner hot plate so I could cook for him while I was there.

We could have eaten all our meals at the Officers Club, but Jerry said the food was terrible and he missed my cooking. I found out how truly bad the food was one morning when we went there for breakfast. Kelly wanted cinnamon toast, but she took one bite and refused to eat any more. When I took a bite to see why she was not eating it, I was shocked. The cook had taken the garlic bread from the night before and sprinkled it with cinnamon! It was rather amazing what I accomplished on that hot plate with an ironing board as my counter space. I remember we had the men from his clinic over for dinner, and I made beef stroganoff. We had no table except a coffee table, so we sat Japanese style on the floor.

What Jerry did not know when he told me to come at that particular time is that it was the monsoon season. It rained twenty-four inches the two months we were there. Jerry had four rooms in the BOQ—bachelor officers' quarters—that were connected, and that is where we lived. Jerry went to work each day, and Kelly and I were left to entertain ourselves. One day I saw a centipede in one of the rooms. It was huge and looked like one of those rubber toys you could buy in the 5&10 cent store. I saw it close to the time Jerry would return to our makeshift home—I thought I would keep an eye on it and let him take care of it. Well, by the time Jerry got there it had vanished. I told Jerry if it touched me, he would have to call for a straitjacket because I would go crazy. We searched and searched for it and could not find it. When we went to bed, I was lying on my stomach in the nude. Jerry was rubbing my back, and all of a sudden, I heard a plop right next to my head.

I thought, *I cannot believe it*, and Jerry yelled, "Get up as fast as you can!"

I jumped up and Jerry turned on the light. Well, here we were on a Marine base with all these Marines who were without their women. There were windows all across the wall, and I was running around with no clothes on.

Jerry kept yelling, "Get down! Get down!" as he tried to capture or kill the centipede.

Finally, he was able to kill it, and we turned off the light and got into bed. I lay there wondering if they traveled in pairs, and it was a long time before I was able to get to sleep.

One morning, Kelly and I were going to go outside for her to play—it was one of the rare days it was not raining. Kelly went out the door, and I turned and went back inside to get something. She was out of my sight for only a few moments, but that was all it took. When I got outside, she was gone—it was like she had vanished into thin air, as the expression goes. I called and called her as I looked for her between the buildings. It was not long before I realized I needed help. I raced up to the street to flag someone down, and who should drive up in a Jeep but the commanding officer of the base and his driver. I was crying as I told him Kelly was missing. Remember, we were on a Marine base, and none of the Marines had their families with them, so Kelly was special to them.

Jerry arrived shortly after I alerted the CO, and I found out later from Jerry that he was with a patient when the CO put his head in the room and said, "Don't get upset but Kelly is missing." And the CO literally called out the Marines. The CO told me later that they were determined to find her, and the Marines were knee deep in mud down the ravines that circled the base when she was found. But Kelly wasn't muddy. She was dry and happy. One of the maids found her playing in another family's quarters. There was one other wife with a little girl about Kelly's age visiting her husband at the same time. They had gone off for the day, and Kelly had opened their door and was playing with the little girl's toys while we all were frantically looking for her. It was a parent's worst nightmare, and it seemed as if she was missing for an eternity, but how blessed we were that it turned out as it did. It has always warmed my heart when I think about all those young Marines swarming the base to find her.

After two months in Okinawa, we spent two weeks traveling around Japan. I returned home to Virginia Beach pregnant. It was August of 1969, and Jerry did not return until early December. Soon after his return, the movers packed up the few things from my apartment, and we got into the car for another cross-country trip to California. Jerry was going to be stationed at the dental clinic at the Navy Base in Alameda.

In those days, the car seats for children were very crude. I am sure in an accident they would not have protected the child but would have become a missile to propel them out of the windshield. We had one of these crude car seats for Kelly's third trip cross-country before she was three years old. We also rigged up a strap with a harness attached so that she could sit or stand but would not be able to move away from the backseat. It was much more secure than the car seat. Every morning we had to drag Kelly kicking and screaming to the car and strap her in. For months after arriving in California, whenever we got into the car and drove a few miles, Kelly would say, "Let's get out and stretch our legs!" Needless to say, it was a long trip to California with a two-year-old who did not like to ride in the car. In fact, we had to be careful she did not get car sick. One time when we had the car seat in the front (we learned to put it in the back after this) and were on a particularly windy road, Kelly turned and threw up all over Jerry!

We rented a house in Alameda. Every day I read about another murder in the area, and even though I had never been fond of dogs, when Jerry suggested we get one, I agreed. A few days later Jerry called me from work and said that his assistant was moving into an apartment where she could not have her dog. The dog was about a year old and was house broken. Did I want to get it? I don't know what came over me, but I said, "Sure."

That evening Sally and her boyfriend, Randy, brought the dog over to our house. The dog's name was Perro. The whole time Sally and Randy sat on the couch, Perro sat at their feet. They said that Perro was very well behaved—he never got on the furniture or chewed anything, but if he did do something we did not want him to do, all we had to do was roll up a piece of newspaper and whack our hand with it.

Sally and Randy were not even out of the driveway when Perro jumped onto the couch! Jerry pulled him off, and he immediately jumped back on. Jerry pulled him off, and he jumped back on. After a few more ons and offs, Jerry rolled up a piece of newspaper and whacked his hand. Perro just sat on the couch and looked at him. Finally, Jerry gave Perro a whack on his hindquarters, and Perro jumped off the couch.

The house was built so that you could go from the living room to the dining room to the kitchen to the entryway to the living room—around in a circle. Perro started running in the circle, defecating as he went—with Jerry chasing him with the rolled-up newspaper. When Jerry finally caught him, Perro wiped his bottom on Jerry's brand-new Desert Boots. (Do you remember those?) They were a light tan suede—I think Jerry ended up throwing them away. We decided it would be best to have Perro sleep in the basement. So, Kelly, Jerry, and I took him downstairs. Jerry put some newspaper on the floor, and Kelly asked her father what the newspaper was for. He told her it was in case Perro needed to tinkle—he would hopefully do it on the paper. I was eight months pregnant.

The next morning while I was fixing breakfast, Jerry went downstairs to get Perro. When he brought him into the kitchen on the leash, Perro was spread eagle on the floor with Jerry dragging him into the room.

When Jerry said, "Leslie, here is your fearless watchdog," I started laughing so hard I started tinkling on the floor as I had no underpants on under my nightgown.

Kelly started jumping up and down saying, "No! No! Mommy—on the newspaper—on the newspaper!!"

When Jerry returned from Okinawa, he was angrier than before he left. There is no doubt Jerry was an angry man. He often told the story of when he was a young boy, and he became angry while he was hammering something. His young puppy was there, and he hit the dog on the head with the hammer. He would laugh and say the dog never walked straight again. Another of his stories was about almost being kicked out of college just before graduation because he had beaten up a fellow student. And then there was the story of his grabbing a professor in dental school by the collar and throwing him against the wall. These stories were all told as if they were funny.

Before Jerry went to Okinawa, his abuse of me was subtle. At least to me it was because it was the type of abuse I had been raised on. Because my mother had verbally abused me all my life, I did not recognize abuse as abuse. It felt familiar. It is what I was accustomed to. After he returned, his abusive words were no longer enough for him. He began to strike out physically.

One night when John was about six months old and Kelly was three, we were all sitting around the dinner table, and I said something Jerry did not like—I cannot imagine what it was, but it infuriated him. He got up from the table, came over to me, grabbed a handful of my hair, dragged me off my chair and shook me all around the dining room. I felt like that little puppy who had been hit on the head with a hammer. He pulled all the hair out in a spot about the size of a fifty-cent piece. He never apologized for anything he did and always told me that I deserved it. It was not until years later when I investigated the trauma I had suffered as a very young child, that I realized I believed him when he told me I had gotten what I deserved—because I had been conditioned to believe it. I really did think I deserved to be abused. These are two things I wrote years later about that time.

Dear John

When you were in my belly
your father gave me a black eye.

You deserve it, he said.

Deserve it?

For carrying your son?

I lie next to him with my eye throbbing
and filling with tears.

And I feel you kicking in protest.

This is my mother—the woman who will give me life.

She deserves it, you say?

———

For Kelly

No, you don't want to come to my house to play.

My daddy hits my mommy.

No, you don't want to come to my house to play.

My mommy is crying.

No, you don't want to come to my house to play.

Can I come to yours?

Chapter 6

First Time

John was born on March 23, 1970. I am amazed when I look back and think about all I did with two little ones—a three-year-old and a newborn baby. I had cocktail parties, dinner parties, dessert parties, and luncheons for the wives of the men in Jerry's department. These were not parties where everyone brought a dish. I did everything myself and did it elegantly. I was a good cook and prepared a delicious meal every night. When Kelly was young, I made many of her clothes and many of mine also. I made Christmas gifts. I decorated the house beautifully for Christmas and made eggs Benedict for Christmas morning. Every morning right after John was born, a friend stopped by after taking her husband to work. She brought doughnuts, and we sat and had doughnuts and coffee. At the time she did not have any children, but when she moved and had her first child, she called me and said, "How did you do it?"

I asked, "What do you mean?"

She said, "How did you get up every morning, get dressed, and have me over for coffee when you had a newborn baby?"

She said that she went days without having time to dress. How did I do it? I do not know. And I was doing all this while in the middle of a very volatile relationship with Jerry.

It took me years and much professional help to realize this—I am a very strong woman. I am a very strong woman who has spent much of her life thinking she was weak. And I thought I was weak because those people closest to me told me I was. Since that was repeated to me from the time I was a tiny child, I did not know any difference.

After Jerry had been home for about a year, he came to me and said he would like to apply for the residency for oral surgery at the Naval Hospital in Oakland. He applied, was accepted, and we bought a sweet little house in San Leandro. Alameda, Oakland, and San Leandro are all in the East Bay area across from San Francisco. It must have been the fall of 1971 that Jerry started his four-year residency. He was older than most of the residents in the medical specialties, so there were many young wives about my age. They may have been around my age, but my children were older because I had been so young when I had Kelly and John. We formed a wonderful group, and since none of us worked outside the home, we did all kinds of things together during the day and also on the weekends with our husbands. There were about ten couples in the group, and because all of us were far away from our families, we celebrated Thanksgiving and Christmas together. It was the first and last time I had such a wonderful circle of friends.

When Jerry finished his residency, he was stationed aboard the *USS Enterprise.* As the time approached for what turned out to be a nine-month cruise, my depression became worse. Jerry talked with a friend who was a resident in psychiatry, and he said I should come in to see him. I think he thought he could talk with me for a session or two and send me on my way. I have no idea what I told him, but after hearing it, he said to me that I needed to see someone. He referred me to the first of a number of psychiatrists I saw in the coming years. I do not remember this man's name, but I do remember he sat way across a big room from me, smoking a pipe.

It is difficult to explain the dynamics of a relationship. There were many insidious ways Jerry used to control me. One thing he did was ask me what I wanted to do about something. I would tell him what I thought, and he would say, "We are not going to do it that way. Here is how we are going to do it." When I would question him on why he had asked me my opinion, he would answer, "I wanted you to feel you had some say in the matter."

Jerry was cruel. He refused to pronounce my name the way I pronounce it. He would not give me gifts for my birthday or Christmas. I would beg him to give me something, no matter how small, just so I would have something to open.

Jerry's birthday is five days before Christmas, and I always gave him many gifts. I kept thinking that by giving to him, he might start giving to me. But it was not until Kelly got older and said to her father, "Okay, we are going out shopping to get presents for Mom," that I began to receive gifts from him, and those were only for Christmas or birthdays.

For years I blamed myself for the problems in our marriage, for the major fights and physical violence, but it wasn't until recently that I realized Jerry would push me and push me, all the while acting like the reasonable one. Then when I became irrational, he would strike out, many times in physically violent ways. He would then tell me it was what I deserved. For years I believed him.

My depression increased as Jerry prepared to leave on the long cruise, but while he was away, I felt free of the tension and control he had over me. When his return home became imminent, my depression worsened again. It became so severe that I planned to kill myself and was hospitalized in a psychiatric facility for two weeks. I remember that when I was taken to the hospital, I had to talk to the admitting psychiatrist. As I sat there answering his questions, I did so with my coat over my head.

The ship was in Hawaii, and Jerry flew home. He had orders to the Naval Hospital in Bethesda, Maryland, and we needed to sell our house in California and buy one in Maryland. My parents were living in Northern Virginia, and my father started looking at the real estate section of *The Washington Post*. He found a house in Rockville, Maryland, and went and looked at it. This was not long after Jerry had gotten home, and I had gotten out of the hospital. My father called and told us he thought this was a great house and one of us should come east to see it. So still feeling shaky and fragile from my hospital stay, I boarded a plane and flew east. I bought the house and flew home to sell our house in California and to get ready to move.

We spent four years in Maryland. While we lived there, I attended Montgomery College in Rockville. It is a two-year college with a lovely campus. Then in my thirties, I was savoring the college experience and making all A's! While writing papers, studying for exams, going to therapy two times a week (and having diarrhea every day I went) taking care of Kelly and John, cooking dinner each night, and taking care of the house, I still entertained. I became good friends with a woman I first met at an elementary school fundraiser. Her two boys and Kelly and John were the same ages, and they, too, became friends. Marsha never got over the fact that I met her and her husband at the fundraiser and then invited them over for dinner. She said she would never have had the nerve to do that. Because I had moved around all my life, I knew the only way I was going to make friends in a new place was to take the initiative. So, I did!

One summer while living in Maryland, we rented a house in Sandbridge, Virginia, with my parents. My sister came from Atlanta, and we were having a lovely family vacation until the day Jerry and I had a horrendous fight over a bread box I had bought. He wanted me to take it back. I said I was leaving, and he blocked the door to the room. I was ready to jump out the window when he said, "Okay but give me your credit cards." I gave them to him, took a bag and put in a summer nighty and a few other things.

All this time John, who was around eight years old, was jumping on the bed yelling, "Mommy, don't leave." I told him I was not leaving *him*—I was leaving his father. But of course, I was leaving everyone. I started walking down the road, and immediately a young man asked me if I wanted a ride. I got into his car, and we drove away. As soon as my sister heard I had left, she jumped on a bike and came looking for me, but I had vanished—into thin air. The young man took me to his house and asked me what I wanted to do. I called the hotline for battered women, and when I told the woman my story, she said they could not help me because I was not from the area. So, I asked the man to take me to the bus station.

I had just enough money for a one-way ticket to Texas with a little left over for vending machine food along the way. My dear friend Judy, from my childhood days of building forts in the woods, lived in Austin. It was a forty-eight-hour bus trip—what an experience! As each mile rolled by, I became happier and happier. I thought— *I do not care if I have to clean motel rooms to live—I've escaped!* The bus stopped in all the little towns, and people got on and off. The smell of liquor permeated the bus—everyone who got on must have been drinking. The second night, the bus driver was a smoker and stopped every hour to have a cigarette. The bus was freezing— he had the air-conditioning turned down so low that I was sitting with my nightgown over my head trying to get warm. I repeatedly asked him to turn it up, and he would say, "Lady, I have a busload of people," meaning everyone else was happy so—shut up about it!

Finally at one of his smoke stops, I yelled back and asked, "Is anyone warm enough on this bus?" No one answered. When he finished his cigarette and got back on, I said, "No one on this bus is warm enough."

He said, "Lady, this is just the outside air."

I calmly reached over and held my hand over the vent. When I said, "I knew this was a long bus ride, but I did not know winter had set in," he didn't say a word. However, he did adjust the air-conditioning.

At another one of his smoke breaks, I decided I had better call and let everyone know I was still alive. They were all still at the beach—my parents, sister, Jerry, and the children. This was long before cell phones. I do not know how I knew the number of the beach house, and I must have reversed the charges because I did not have any money. All Jerry was worried about was that he wanted me to come back before they went home to Maryland because he did not want the neighbors to wonder why he had returned without me. Well, there was no way that could happen because I was in the middle of nowhere with no money. So, I got back on the bus and continued on to Texas.

I must have called Judy somewhere along the way because she was waiting for me when I finally arrived and staggered off the bus. Judy and I had lost touch with each other, but we had recently reconnected, and she had just visited us in Maryland. If we had not reconnected at that time, I do not know where I would have gone.

Judy lived in a house with a number of other people—all a little strange by the standards of this suburban housewife. There was one young woman I can remember vividly. She had a very technical job dealing with computer chips, and she did this while being totally stoned. She worked from home and started smoking pot first thing in the morning and smoked it all day long. I asked Judy how this woman was able to function, and Judy told me the woman said it helped her concentrate. Judy and her interesting group of roommates introduced me to smoking pot. It certainly did *not* help me concentrate. I just got mellow and sleepy. Judy was trying to convince me to stay and not go back to Jerry, and Jerry was calling and trying to get me to come home.

This was the first time I left him, but I left him numerous times after this, and each time he said the things I so wanted to hear from him—the things he would not say when I was there with him. He would tell me how important I was to him, how much he loved me, and how sorry he was. He always promised he would never again abuse me. I would believe him and go back.

This time, I stayed about a week with Judy before Jerry convinced me to come home. Because I had no money and no credit cards, Jerry made the reservations for me to fly home. When I got on the plane, I had two big joints in my suitcase! My parents, who lived in Northern Virginia near the airport, picked me up, and I stayed a few days with them before going home. Since I could not take the joints back home with me, I had to smoke them before I left.

My parents went out two of the nights I was there, and I sat on their deck each of those nights and smoked a whole joint by myself. Boy did I get high, and boy did it feel good! I remember how everything looked different. Their deck was off the second story of their house and was surrounded by many tall trees. By the time I had finished smoking the first joint, the leaves of the trees looked like hands clapping. I felt as if they were clapping for me, cheering me on, but I was so lost and disconnected from myself that I did not know what they would be cheering about. On the outside, I appeared totally put together. But on the inside, I was empty. I had never been celebrated by anyone in my life.

We are all born with self-esteem. Mine had been slowly eroded from the time I was an infant. Now, in my thirties, my mother was still saying disparaging things to me, as was my husband. I believed what they said because I had never been told anything that would negate their negative opinions of me.

Once I was back home, of course, nothing changed. The abuse continued. The Sunday Kelly was to be confirmed at church, my parents were coming to our house to go with us. When they arrived, I walked downstairs with blood running down my face from a cut above my eye. I drove myself to the emergency room while they all went to church for Kelly's big day. I met them at the restaurant for brunch with a black eye and a big bandage. We sat there and ate as if nothing had happened. Not one word was ever spoken about it. Because I was getting no support from my parents, I decided to call one of Jerry's sisters in Tennessee. Jerry had three sisters and two brothers. The sister I called was the one we were both closest to. She and one of his brothers came and stayed with us for a couple of days during which they tried to talk to Jerry about his violent behavior, but Jerry was very angry and closed off, and nothing came of their "intervention."

This is what happened when I told my mother about Jerry's abuse.

Please Help

I told my mother that my husband hit me.

She said nothing.

I was hoping for a sign—a word—an outrage
that this was a terrible thing.

But she said nothing.

Maybe I do deserve it.

Maybe I will go on pretending that my
marriage is wonderful—the perfect
little family.

I reached out to my mother for help.

But she said nothing.

And that was the most silent silence I have ever heard.

Chapter 7

It Is Time to Leave

After living four years in Maryland, Jerry was transferred to the Naval Hospital in Portsmouth, Virginia. We bought a lovely new house in Virginia Beach, where my parents were now living. The house backed up to a wetlands area that was a riot of pink in the spring when the mountain laurel was in bloom. We had a large deck built, and I filled it with pots of flowers. I have always been very creative, and I decorated this house beautifully. Interestingly, I can take whatever furniture and accessories I have and make them work in an attractive way.

When we moved to Virginia Beach, we bought a beautiful sailboat—a thirty-foot O'Day. We were right there where the Chesapeake Bay meets the Atlantic Ocean, and we had many sailing adventures on the bay. We kept our boat at the Naval Station in Norfolk, and one day a submarine came right up next to us. They were so close that we could see that the crew was not happy about us being as close as we were. I loved being on the water. Sailing is special because it is quiet and therefore peaceful, unless you are in a storm or heavy winds, and then it is very exciting! We would find a spot to anchor for the night. After the sails were down and the anchor was set, we would sit with a drink and watch the day slowly turn to night. Often, we would see the water birds flying home to roost. A charcoal grill attached to the stern railing enabled us to have many delicious dinners. Then after a good dinner and a game of Scrabble, we were rocked to sleep in the forward cabin with the cool air blowing into the hatch. When my parents took a cruise to Bermuda out of Norfolk, we followed their ship and waved goodbye.

Being on the boat was either peaceful or exciting, depending on the weather. This could also be said about my marriage. It could be peaceful and fun, and then suddenly it could turn horrifying. One of my most terrifying memories is from one summer on the boat. Jerry, our son, John, who must have been thirteen years old at the time, my sister Deborah, and I took a weeklong cruise on the bay. We were having a wonderful time until one day Jerry asked John to hold the boat away from the dock. John was a skinny little kid, and the boat weighed over ten thousand pounds, so it isn't hard to understand why John was unable to do it. But that did not matter to Jerry—he became so incensed that he grabbed John, pulled him onto the boat and started beating his head on the winch, which is a big round metal thingamajig used to trim the sails. My sister and I stood there paralyzed as Jerry continued to beat John's head against the winch and the boat bang, bang, banged against the dock. We did not intervene. We did not even yell at him to stop. We just stood there and watched. What happened next? I cannot remember. I think the whole thing was so shocking that all I can remember is the horror of it—not what happened immediately afterward. I do know we went on with our trip, and as with all of the other horrors in the family, nothing was ever said about it. This memory is so horrific that I have told this story to very few people. It makes me realize how beaten down I was because I believe this would have been the final straw for most other mothers. They would have taken their children and left. I stayed.

Later on, when Kelly was away in college, and John was in high school, I sensed something was going on with Jerry. He became serious about losing weight. He constantly talked about the class he was taking at the gym during lunch. I found out what was going on when I was preparing dinner for my parents and their good friends, the Foxes. My parents had just returned from an extended trip to China, and it was my mother's birthday.

That afternoon as I was getting everything ready for the evening, Jerry came into the kitchen and announced that he had been having an affair with a young woman he met in that gym class. And she was young, especially next to Jerry's fifty. She was just two years older than Kelly, who was twenty at the time. He proceeded to tell me all the details. Her husband was in a residency for psychiatry, and they were not going to the gym but were having sex at her house every day during lunch time. He tried to justify the affair by saying that I had gained a little weight—I had always been very thin and though I'd gained a couple of pounds would still probably have been deemed underweight. Another reason was there was some hair on the bathroom floor—how crazy is that? The big reason he said was he wanted to see if he could satisfy a younger woman. I replied with the only sane thing I could muster: "I would think it would be more important to know if you could still satisfy the woman you have been married to for twenty-two years."

Jerry had done it again. He'd turned my life upside down moments before my parents and the Foxes arrived for dinner. As hateful and abusive as Jerry could be, I never thought he would have an affair. He was always derogatory about any man he knew who was being unfaithful to his wife. I sat through that dinner with tears streaming down my face, and no one said a word. As was typical for my parents—they did not want to know. No one hugged me and asked what was wrong. I just served a beautiful dinner while crying, then wished them a good night and turned around to enter the nightmare Jerry had created. Jerry could not understand why he could not continue to be "friends" with Laura.

One story he told me was that her sister had been killed by an ex-boyfriend when she was in bed with a new boyfriend, and Jerry thought Laura was trying to recreate that scenario with him. Every lunchtime, he and she were in her marriage bed having sex. Her husband could have come home at any time. He told me Laura had been driving by our house. I did not know what she looked like, but she knew who I was because we had been to the same parties. I immediately started going to a counselor, and she tried to go to the same counselor. Luckily, he realized who she was and told her he could not see her. Again, I stayed.

We stayed together two more years. In that time Jerry retired from the Navy, but he did not know what he wanted to do next. Suddenly, he decided he wanted to move onto a sailboat and travel. I agreed, and we started giving things away as we began planning to sell everything else. It was at this time that I finally woke up. Anytime I disagreed with Jerry, he would get extremely angry and tell me that I had never supported him in anything he wanted to do. The light bulb *finally* went on—for all the twenty-plus years of our marriage, my mind was in such turmoil that it took me that long to see things as they were. I realized I had supported him in *everything* he had wanted to do—going back into the Navy, doing a residency in oral maxillofacial surgery, and now selling all our things and moving onto a sailboat! Jerry had always used that attack to make me get back into line, to make me not have an opinion of my own. I say the "light bulb *finally* went on," but it was still very dim. I was just beginning to wake up and realize how wrong all of this was.

He changed his mind about moving on a boat and decided to buy an oral surgery practice in Williamsburg, Virginia. Again, I supported him. We started building a home in Kingsmill, one of the lovely gated communities in Williamsburg. I applied to the College of William & Mary and was accepted as one of its few part-time students. I loved Williamsburg, but for Jerry, the happier and healthier I became, the angrier and more volatile he got. He complained about my depression and my crying, but it was much easier for him to manipulate me when I was depressed and weak. Then the woman he had had the affair with started sending him letters, and he could not understand why I was against him having a relationship with her.

It was the end of 1989, and we went to Maryland to visit friends for the New Year's holiday. As we were lying in bed the night before going home the next day, Jerry told me he wanted a divorce, that he had never loved me. That, I think is probably true—he *had* never loved me. Love does not manifest itself in abuse. Trying in my mind to put his "I never loved you" with the fact that in spite of his affair, he was very physically attracted to me, I said in response, "We did have a good sex life though, didn't we?"

And Jerry replied, "Making love to you is like making love to a dead person. The only way I know you are alive is that I can hear your heartbeat." It was at that very moment I said to myself—*I will never allow this man to say anything else to me again.*

Of all the terrible things he had done to me over the years—to me this was so ugly and hateful that I was finally determined to leave and not return. We had to drive four hours home, and all the way home Jerry berated me, telling me what a horrible person I was, telling me I would have nothing—everything was his because he had made the money.

When we arrived back in Williamsburg, I threw my suitcase into the trunk of my car and drove to my parents' house in Virginia Beach. On the way I stopped by the bank and withdrew all the money in our checking account—$25,000. That was far more than we usually had in our account, but we had just sold our house in Virginia Beach. Jerry did not find out about it until he wrote a check for the mortgage, and the bank called him to inform him there was no money in the account. He was still furious about it three years later when our divorce was finalized.

At the time, my mother was in Colorado with my brother and sister-in-law who had just had their first baby on Christmas Eve. I had overheard my father telling someone he finally had a real grandchild—what were my two children, and what about my sister's two children? He didn't consider them "real" because they were not Keegans?

Dear Old Dad

Hey! Dad, I heard you.

What did you think?
I wouldn't hear.
Or didn't you care?

Well, I *did* hear you
telling everyone
when David's son Cobun was born
that you finally had a *real* grandchild.

A *real* grandchild?

What about
      Kelly
      John
      Kennedy and
      Keith

What are they?
Faux grandchildren?

I know people with adopted grandchildren
of a different race
who call them their own.

But you
you call your flesh and blood
fakes, frauds, imposters.

Because they are the progeny
of your daughters
not of your son.

So, my mother was in Colorado, and my father and I were alone in their house in Virginia Beach. Every morning, my father would get up and say things like, "Leslie, I know why Jerry had that affair. He was trying to get rid of you," or, "Leslie, we do not know that Jerry abused you. It is all hearsay."

"Dad," I said, "you saw the blood running down my face."

To which he replied, "You could have walked into a doorknob."

Those were his exact words. I was making many phone calls to set up accounts for myself and find out what I had to do to live on my own. I got off the phone after one of my calls, and my father said, "Leslie, you said *okay* twenty-four times on that call. Twenty-four times! I went to Toastmasters to learn how to give speeches, and they said to never say *okay*."

I replied, "Okay, Dad." But it went right over his head—he was too intent on telling me how wrong I had been to hear what I had said.

One night Jerry drove from Williamsburg and appeared at my father's front door. There was a panel of glass next to the door so I could see him standing there. As he kept trying to talk to me, I would say, "If you do not leave, I am calling the police."

I repeated it many times, and finally Jerry said, "Let me talk with Earl."

Earl was my father, and again I said, "I am going to call the police."

Finally, Jerry turned to leave, and I walked into the kitchen to find my father sitting on the floor, hiding.

He said in a frightened voice, "I don't want to talk to Jerry. I don't want to talk to Jerry."

I looked at my father, shook my head and said, "Don't worry. You do not have to talk to him. He is leaving."

A few nights later, I was sitting and reading in my parents' family room at two o'clock in the morning. I was facing the room's large bay window. All of a sudden, I heard three loud bangs that to me sounded like gunshots. I jumped up and ran out of the room so fast that it felt as if my feet were not touching the floor. I ran into my father's bedroom, yelling, "I think Jerry is shooting at me!"

I grabbed the phone and dialed 911. When the dispatcher answered, I could hardly speak as I told her I thought my husband was shooting at me. I was able to give her the information, and she told me to stay on the line until the police arrived. She heard my father say that he was going to go out and investigate, and she told me to tell him to stay where he was. This was the man who a few nights before had been hiding on the kitchen floor afraid he was going to have to talk to Jerry, and now he was going outside to check and see if Jerry was out there shooting at the house.

The police arrived and walked around the house. Coming back inside they said that someone had thrown three eggs against the bay window. Whoever it was had found the most vulnerable person in the neighborhood and frightened her beyond words. They must have had a great laugh seeing me flee from the room. The officers were wonderful to me—far better than my own father. To see if Jerry was in Williamsburg, one officer called him, waking him up before saying to him he must have the wrong number.

Jerry was calling me repeatedly. This was a time before cell phones or even portable phones or caller ID. Each time I answered and heard Jerry's voice, I would say, "If you have anything you need to tell me, call my lawyer." He also sent many letters to my post office box. I never opened any of them. I sent them to my attorney unopened. I knew from all the other times I had tried to leave that if I let him talk to me, I would return. This time I was determined that was *not* going to happen.

Many women have said to me that they would leave the first time they were hit. I was lucky my children were grown and that I had some money, but this is how I imagine it would be for a woman who had young children and no money and no place to go.

All He Would Have to do Is Hit Me One Time

The first time he hit me—I would be out of there, you say?

Oh, really, and where would you go?

Are your children going with you?

Quick! Pack your bags kids—we're leaving. No, you can't take your Nintendo, and the hamster must stay. No, forget about your science project, and we can't take your new bike. Come on kids— Hurry! Hurry! Don't forget your socks. And yes, throw in your wet bathing suit. Hurry! Hurry! We have to leave before Dad gets home. Stop crying—we don't have time.

Mom, what about my tooth—the one I was going to put under my pillow?

Oh, Lord, will the Tooth Fairy have any money to give?

No, you don't have time to find your teddy bear. It's time to go.

Throw it in the car, kids.

We have to get out of here.

Mom, where are we going?

I don't know. Do you have any money in your piggy bank?

Chapter 8:

Finding My Truth

My mother called me and said Jerry had written a letter to my father. She wanted to read it to me, but I asked her not to, explaining that if I was going to do this, I could not hear things like that. My mother totally ignored me and started reading.

I kept repeating, "I don't want to hear it! I don't want to hear it!" until my mother, in a rage, slammed down the phone.

I happened to have an appointment with the psychologist I was seeing, and as I was sitting in his waiting room, I started crying from the deepest part of me. I sounded like a wounded animal and that is what I was—a wounded animal. I know this is hard to believe but that was the first time I had ever said *no* to my mother. I realized as a young child what would happen if I said *no*, and I was right. There was *no* saying *no* to her.

From the time I was that little toddler sitting on the ottoman so petrified of my mother that I did not move, I knew I could not disagree with her or even ask her to honor my wishes. Her favorite thing to do to me when I was a teenager and was excited about going out with my friends was to tell me I could not go. She would use some minor or imagined infraction I had incurred to punish me. My reaction was to immediately start wailing and begging her to change her mind. Upon hearing me, my sister Deborah swore she would never act that way, but I had no shame. My mother usually relented and allowed me to go. So often, I went out with red, swollen eyes. This time I was so determined to leave Jerry that I risked going against my mother. I knew that to cross my mother would have dire circumstances. It would unleash her fury, and she would turn against me. But this is something I had to do.

A court date was coming up to determine temporary support for me until we divorced. My sister Deborah made my father promise he would be there for me. He had planned to go out to Colorado to be with my mother, brother, sister-in-law, and his "first real grandchild." But he promised my sister he would delay his trip until after the court date. My sister told him that if he would not be there for me, she would take time off from her job and fly up from Atlanta to be there. She did not want me to have to face Jerry alone. My brother, David, who was a flight attendant, came through Virginia Beach on one of his trips. Unbeknownst to my sister and me, my brother convinced my father that I did not need him there during the hearing. My father did not tell me he was leaving. He told the waitress in the restaurant where my brother and I were having lunch with him. That is how my father let me know he would not be there. He told the waitress that in two days he was flying to Colorado to see his "first real grandchild." I did not say anything but avoided him the whole next day by leaving the house. When I got home that evening, he told me that I was going to have to get up at five o'clock to drive him to the airport. All I said was *okay*.

The next morning when I got to the garage, my father had put his suitcase in the trunk of his car. He drove a big red Cadillac, and I drove a much smaller Mercedes. All I said to him was, "Dad, I would rather drive my car."

Acting totally put out, he huffed and puffed as he put his suitcase in my car. It was a quiet ride to the airport. I felt totally abandoned by my parents. It was beyond my comprehension that the first time

I heard my father was flying to Colorado was when he told a waitress. I was emotionally fragile. My sister was a teacher and was not able to come. I was alone. For a number of years, I had unsuccessfully tried to leave Jerry. This was a monumental attempt to free myself from a toxic, abusive marriage. I felt as if a giant magnet was pulling me back. As determined as I was this time, I still did not know if I could be successful.

That night after dropping my father at the airport earlier, I was alone in my parents' house, and it was pouring rain. I started the dishwasher and left the kitchen. A little while later I walked back into the kitchen and water was gushing out of the dishwasher all over the new wooden floor. I quickly turned the dishwasher off, but the water kept coming. My parents had just gotten city water after years of having a well, and I did not know where the turn-off was. I called my father in Colorado. He told me where it was and that he would stay on the line. I had to go out into what was a torrential downpour, get down in the mud, and reach down into a hole to turn off the valve. Luckily, the entryway was slate—so I was able to take my clothes off before walking across the new carpet to the kitchen. When I picked up the phone, my father immediately started yelling at me.

"Do you mean to tell me I have been gone only a day and you are already running the dishwasher?"

I said, "Goodbye, Dad," and I hung up.

My mother started calling and, because I did not answer, she left an angry, nasty message that I was to call the plumber the next day and I was to clean up the mess in the kitchen.

I don't remember how I cleaned up the water, but I do know I packed my bag that night and was ready to leave the next morning. As I was getting ready to walk out the door, my parents' neighbor, Ruth, came in and said, "Leslie, you owe your parents an apology, and they want you to call the plumber."

I said, "Ruth, I am leaving, and they can call the plumber when they return from Colorado."

Ruth also told me that my father had cried all the way to Colorado because I had been so hateful to him. The "hateful" thing I did was telling him I wanted to drive my car to the airport instead of his.

And where was I going? At first, I had no idea. I just knew I could not stay where I was. Looking back, I can see the Universe was supporting me. I did not realize it then, but I can see it now. At that time, I did not pray; I did not even go to church, but the night everything fell apart with my parents, I called the woman who cut my hair. Now I see that I was led to call her because she had the perfect solution for me. She told me she and Paul were living together in her apartment. But Paul had a completely furnished condo that he would be willing to rent to me. I took my suitcase that day, met Paul at the condo and moved in. I did not even have to buy a dish towel. Everything I needed was there, waiting for me!

My parents were not only *not* supporting me, but they were also abusing me—my father with his nasty comments at breakfast and my mother by not honoring my requests. I finally realized why I had let myself be abused for those twenty-four years of my marriage. It felt familiar. It is what I was accustomed to. My parents were *not* loving parents. By leaving Jerry and saying I would no longer consent to being treated that way, I was upsetting the fragile balance of my toxic birth family. My parents were lashing out, and it felt to me as if they were thinking, *Jerry did not completely destroy her, let's see if we can finish the job.*

I think I would have committed suicide if I had stayed and allowed my parents to continue their abuse. To have any chance of becoming mentally healthy, I had to leave. I knew if I did not leave my parents, I would not survive. So, I left Jerry in January and my parents in February.

That was the last time I spoke to my father for twenty-six years, though I did see him at least three times during that time span. Once, I was in a bakery having coffee with a friend. I could hear him come in the front door. There was no mistaking his loud voice full of bravado. I told my friend I had to leave, and, in my leaving, I had to walk past him. He called out my name, but I just kept walking.

It is interesting how life unfolds. The next time I was driving to school on a route I never went on. I had taken it because the road I usually took was having major repair work done. It was pouring rain, and my father was standing by the side of the road under an umbrella—it appeared as if his car had broken down. I just drove by and did not look back.

The third time, he was sitting in his car outside a grocery store, and I assumed he was waiting for my mother. I suddenly decided there were plenty of other grocery stores I could go to. I was criticized by many for my decision to no longer have anything to do with my parents, but I never regretted it. In fact, I do not think I would be here today if I had stayed and let them treat me the way they had treated me for forty-four years.

My parents became very close to Jerry, even visiting him in Florida when he moved there. They went around Virginia Beach telling people what a fine person he was. I went to the dental hygienist one day, and she said to me that my mother had just been in and was talking about Jerry. The hygienist could not understand why I had left him. Evidently, my mother had gone on and on about what a wonderful person he was.

No, I have never regretted my decision, and I never went back to that hygienist.

Though I don't regret my decision, none of it was easy. Within a span of two months, I lost everything—my marriage, my parents, all my beautiful things, and many of the friends we had as a couple.

I ended up in a psychiatric hospital for two weeks and went to an aftercare program for six weeks after being released. I had been going to the psychologist I started seeing when Jerry had the affair two years before. I was also seeing a psychiatrist for med-checks. Dr. P had put me on an antidepressant, and I went to talk to him for fifteen minutes at regular intervals. On the visit right before I went into the hospital, I heard a whisper in my right ear that said, "This man will hear what you have been trying to say." I did not know it at the time, but I now know that was my spirit guide telling me this was the doctor I needed to see. Had I not listened, I would not have had the chance to heal.

I didn't even know what I had been trying to say because the sub-conscious talks in code. I had suffered so much trauma pre-verbal (or before I was able to speak), and I was an expert at what I called "going away" or dissociation. Therefore, I needed someone to help me uncover the reasons for my severe depression—they were hidden in my subconscious. I had been in therapy for fourteen years with three different doctors, including the psychologist I was seeing at the time. Each one of them had helped me in some way to get ready to do the hard work with Dr. P.

I had to expose the deepest traumas if I was going to completely heal. It is extremely painful when these psychic traumas are uncov-ered. I needed someone who was an expert at pulling out the hidden stories and at the same time giving me the support I would need to face the frightening unknown. I asked Dr. P if I could be his patient.

He looked out the window for what seemed like a long time before he answered, "Yes, I will see you as a patient."

A number of years later, I asked him why he had waited so long before answering me, and he said, "Because I knew I would have to travel a long, hard road with you, and I was wondering if I was up to doing it."

Thank goodness he said yes because he was an expert at deciphering my code. I would go in to see him and start telling one story after another—about a movie I had seen, a book I was reading, a conversation with a friend for example—and he would sit quietly for a few minutes and then tell me how all the stories were saying the same thing. They all had the same theme.

Psychotherapy is much like peeling an onion. These stories may not have seemed to mean anything significant at the time, but each theme of each session exposed another layer until we arrived at the core of my injuries. I always told people that Dr. P was very hard on me. But I kept going back week after week because I was determined not to live the rest of my life in the mental hell I had lived in since I was a child.

Dr. P did make me see the truth. I say he *made* me but what he did was offer the truth to me, and it was my decision on whether or not to take it. During one session when I was strong enough to hear it, Dr. P said, "If you will believe this, everything else will make sense. Your parents never loved you." That was an extremely hard thing to hear, but he was right—it did make everything they had done to me make sense.

Dr. P also told me that if I had had one person to support, nurture, or believe in me—like a teacher, grandparent, older neighbor—I would not be in his office. Recently, I took a workshop, and the facilitator said the same thing. He said research has shown we need just one person to believe in us for us to be emotionally healthy. I had no one. We left my loving grandmother and godmother when I was five. We moved constantly, never giving me a chance to form a lasting relationship with anyone.

Even at this time I was very much alone. My sister Deborah has always been there for me. She decided she wanted to stay close to my parents and close to me, which she did. However, at this time she was busy with her career and lived six hundred miles away in Atlanta. My sister Melanie and I loved each other but had never been close. My brother was furious at me for leaving our parents, and to this day despises me. I had a few friends but no one I was particularly close to. It is only now as I look back that I realize how much strength it took for me to do what I did.

And where did that strength come from?

I now believe that the Universe was supporting me. When I needed a place to live, a beautifully appointed condo appeared. When I was ready for the right doctor to help me heal, Dr. P appeared. So even though the outer world had constantly eroded my confidence, I had an inner strength that gave me the courage to leave everything behind and step out into the unknown. I now know that inner strength came from the Universe. I had God, the angels, my spirit guide, and many more spiritual beings by my side supporting me, holding me up when I felt there was no ground beneath my feet.

It certainly wasn't easy. As I have said, I ended up in a psychiatric hospital, but that had more to do with the mental state I had been in most of my life. Leaving just exacerbated my fragile mental state. I lost weight because I had trouble eating. I could not sleep at night. Each night I would lie on the couch and listen over and over again to the music soundtrack to the movie *Working Girl.* When I was sitting there in the condo alone at night, I felt as if I had to hang on tightly to the couch to keep myself from going back. It would have been easy to do because with his phone calls and letters, Jerry was trying to get me to come back. But I knew that would be the death of me, and when I say "the death of me," I mean I would have had to give up having the chance to become the person I was meant to be. And again, I had no idea who or what that was. It was just a know-ing, a knowing that I was not meant to be this unhappy, depressed person I had been all my life up to this moment, this person who allowed others to abuse her, this person who never spoke her truth, this person who let others define her.

So, what was helping me during this terribly difficult time of leav-ing my marriage, my parents, and uncovering the traumas of my childhood? I think it was that I was going to school. After leaving Jerry, I transferred from the College of William & Mary to Old Dominion University in Norfolk, Virginia. I did not want to stay in the same town where Jerry was living and practicing oral surgery. I had always wanted to earn a college degree, and this was the perfect time for me to do so. I loved going to school! I immersed myself in my studies, and as I was able to do all my life, I could accomplish much even as all the drama and trauma was swirling around and through me.

I majored in psychology and minored in criminal justice. The first semester at Old Dominion, I was taking a class on victims of crime. The night after the first class, I sat down to read the assignment in the text. All of a sudden, a poem on abuse flowed through me completely written. I wrote it down and went back to reading. Another poem flowed through me. I sat there for hours reading and writing down the poems. This poem on starting to live is one of the poems that came through me that night.

Starting to Live

All I have ever known is abuse
from those I thought would love me.

As a little child, I reached out
for love.

It was not there.

When I reached out
and there was nothing
I lost my balance.

That is not all I lost.

I lost my childhood.

I lost myself.

But there was a tiny ember
that did not go out.

Oh, there were times when it was
so very minute it could not be seen.

But it was there
waiting.

Waiting until I had the courage
to face the truth.

To face the truth and not die.

Because only by facing the truth
could I start to live.

And nurture
the ember into a flame.

Part II:
Into the Light

Chapter 9

A New Life

It was February 1992. I had been living alone and going to school for two years. This semester I had an early morning class. Each morning I would meet my friend Pam for breakfast in the Student Union cafeteria. One morning when Pam got up for something, a man came over and said, "Are you a teacher?"

I said, "No, I am a student."

He said, "No, I mean in the public school system. You look familiar." We chatted for a few minutes, and he left.

When Pam got back, she said, "What did he want?" I told her he said that I looked familiar.

Pam replied, "Oh, Leslie, that is the oldest line in the book!"

That afternoon I was in the Student Union cafeteria by myself, and the man came along again. This time he was dressed in a tuxedo. The man, John, was a professional musician. He played the bass trombone, and he was playing in the Barnum and Bailey Circus band while it was in town. Much later, he told me he had purposely gone home and changed and then came back looking for me because he thought no woman could resist a man in a tuxedo. Well, I guess that was true in this case because we ended up living together for twenty-four years! We never married but always said we were married without the paperwork.

John had been teaching strings (he also played the cello) in the public school system in Norfolk under a special license because he did not have a degree in music. When I met him, he had taken a leave of absence to finish his degree. He was a man in his fifties, in the middle of getting a divorce, had no job and no money. He had just declared bankruptcy and lost his house. When I divorced, I let Jerry have everything—the house, the beautiful antiques we had acquired over the years—everything. I got a small cash settlement and some of his retirement from the military.

So, John and I had very little, but obviously for me, possessions were not important, or I would not have left everything behind. I had always been happy with whatever I had, never feeling I had to have more. And possessions had never been important to John. He drove a horrible old car, had two sport coats, a couple of pairs of pants, a pair of black shoes, a pair of brown shoes, a pair of tennis shoes, and, of course, his tuxedo! From his marriage, we got an old couch and two old dressers.

We had no possessions, but we also had no drama, no fighting, no violence. Our life together was peaceful. John was so happy to have me in his life, and I felt the same way about him. We were kind to each other. No matter how many possessions Jerry and I had, it was never enough for him. No matter how much I did, it was never enough for him. Jerry had a beautiful, devoted wife, but that was not enough. He had to have an affair to prove something to himself. And Jerry was angry he had to work. However, when he retired from the Navy, he no longer had to work but chose to go into private practice. We could have lived on his retirement, but it would have been a simpler life, not a life Jerry wanted to live.

John was happy with a simple life as long as he had his music. John was always thinking about little things he could do for me. Jerry never even wanted to buy me a birthday or Christmas present. After

I Am the Whisper of the Wind

my divorce from Jerry, I stopped cooking dinner. John was fine with that. At that time in Norfolk, there were many places we could have a nice dinner for not much money. That is what we did each night. I would occasionally cook something simple like a pot of soup, but it was when I felt like it, not because I had to do it.

When John started teaching again, he wore a coat and tie each day, and I told him I was not willing to iron his shirts. He was fine with that and took them to a laundry. We did not have any children at home. Kelly was married the October of the year I left her father. My son, John, had dropped out of high school and moved to Colorado to live with my brother a couple of years before I left. My new partner, John, had three grown children living in California and two younger children living with their mother in North Carolina. Having no children at home, we were able to just concentrate on each other.

When John finished his degree almost two years after we started living together, he returned to his teaching job and then we had more money. After living a number of years in an old apartment, we bought an old condo. The only reason we were able to do this is that the owners wanted to finance it. We were very lucky because a bank would not have considered us for a loan with John's bankruptcy and our meager finances. From the time we started living together, John and I did not celebrate Christmas in the traditional way. None of our children ever invited us to join them for the holidays, so John and I often looked at each other and said, "It's just you and me, babe."

Those first few years when we had little money, we went out for a nice Christmas dinner. Then, when John started teaching, we decided to go away for the ten days he had off. When we lived in Norfolk, we went to Bethany Beach, Delaware, and rented a condo on the ocean.

By this time, I had not been seeing Dr. P for a number of years. I had seen him once a week for the two years before I met John, and

I continued to see him for two more years after we met. In that time Dr. P had gone back into the Navy. I was able to continue seeing him because I had been married to Jerry for over twenty years of his active-duty service, and therefore, I had military medical privileges. Unfortunately, Dr. P and I had to suddenly terminate our time together when he received emergency orders to move to Spain. He called me and told me he was leaving. We never had a proper ending to our relationship. Luckily, by this time I was, as he told me, one of only two people in all of the many people he had treated who had been able to overcome the issues inhibiting their mental well-being.

In order to become mentally healthy, I had to experience the fear and pain I had blocked myself from feeling when I was abused by my mother as a child. I had to stop reliving all the hateful things she and others had done to me. I had thought that by going to therapy, I would one day never feel pain or depression again. Then in one of our sessions, I realized that by becoming mentally healthy I was going to feel pain and sorrow, but I was going to feel them when it was appropriate to do so. What Dr. P had helped me to do was get in touch with my traumatic experiences and feel the feelings I had suppressed surrounding those events. I had to feel them to heal them. Only by doing so was I able to begin to feel happiness.

My most important insight was that there is joy on the other side of the pain. In order to start living a happy, joy-filled life, I had to allow myself to feel the feelings I had suppressed when the events occurred. My depression lifted and I felt lighter and began to enjoy each day. That is not to say I never feel depressed anymore. But when I do, it does not last long.

In about 1999, we started going to Maine for two weeks at the end of the summer just before school started for John in September. In the winter of 2000 or 2001, I promised myself I would live in New England before I died. I thought to myself that I would probably have to wait until John died because he had always lived in Norfolk where he had a very active musical life. I never imagined he would ever want to leave. I did not tell anyone about this promise I had made to myself. John retired in June of 2002, and when we were in Maine that August, he turned to me and said, "Let's move here. We could never live in a more beautiful place."

I couldn't believe it! I had put it out there to the Universe, and the Universe had answered! We got back to Norfolk the first week in September, sold our condo, packed up everything and were back in Maine the third week in October!

I found a house for rent in the newspaper, and when we went to see it, we rented it right away. It was a funky yellow house that had been built as a summer house and had strange things like hot water in one of the toilets. But it had a magnificent view of the Union River Bay with a rocky beach just beyond the backyard. I was so happy there. I was living in New England, a place I had wanted to live in since I lived in Rhode Island when I was fifteen. I was surrounded by the beauty of nature, which had always been the thing that fed my soul.

It snowed the day we moved in and snowed a lot that winter. Every morning I would go out to the shed that housed the firewood, fill up a wheelbarrow with wood, and take it into the house where we would have a fire lit all day while looking out at that wonderful view. When summer came, we walked along the shore and found all kinds of interesting rocks. The story we heard was that when the glaciers came down to Maine, they picked up rocks on their journey from the north. When they retreated, they dropped the rocks in Maine. One evening we went down to the bay. For some reason, I turned over one of the rocks right along the water's edge. Underneath, there were three or four tiny starfish. I turned the rock back over and started looking under other rocks, finding baby starfish under each one. What caused me to look under the first one? Now, as I think about it, I believe I was guided by the Universe to go down to the river that night and guided to turn that first rock over because for me this became a very spiritual experience. I felt connected to that mother who had scattered her babies along the shore. Here is a poem I wrote about that time. To me, it shows that my happiness is always mingled with a sense of melancholy.

Teary Hopeful

As I walk on the uneven shore
large rocks obstruct my way.

It is that time before the moon appears
dark and quiet.

The only sound the gentle lapping of the water.

Looking out across the bay
I see the moon begin its slow ascent.

So so slow
until it pops up out of the trees.

The full moon bright
its edges blurry through my tears.

On a whim I make a wish
and wonder: Do wishes come true?

Can I teach myself to value what I have?

As if I had much.

As if I would live forever.

I absolutely loved living there in that funky house on the bay. But after ten months, the owner came and wanted to raise the rent 50 percent. He said he was either going to do that or turn it into a summer rental. I was devastated.

We had become friends with the next-door neighbors, and they said, "Why don't you move into mom and dad's house across the road. We are moving them down here, so we can take care of them. We will never sell the house, so you can live there for as long as you want."

We lived in this house they "were never going to sell" for ten months. Then after we had painted, bought things to go into the house, had the house thoroughly cleaned and dragged a lot of trash out of the backyard, they came and said they had sold the house. I immediately started crying—and I didn't even like that big old house. It was just that I did not want to be forced to move again.

We started looking for another place to rent. John and I had decided when we arrived in Maine that we did not want to buy a house, but what we did not know is how hard it would be to find year-round, long-term rentals. Many people use their properties as summer rentals—they can make much more money renting them by the week in the summer—and Maine has a short summer!

John started calling around looking for another place to live. We were living in Surry but decided since we had to move, we would like to move to Blue Hill. While living in Surry, we became active in the Blue Hill library group that had movies on the weekend and play readings once a month. But John was having no success in his search, and I was so disappointed and angry.

Since I was no longer in therapy, I did not have someone to help me see that being forced to move was triggering the feelings I had as a child. It is only by looking back that I realize this is what I felt when I was a child forced to move, having no voice in what happened to me. As a child, all I did was cry about the situation.

Now, poor John was the recipient of my past and present anger. I was a bitch to live with. John was patient and kind to me, knowing this was not my normal way of being—that I was angry about the situation. He gave me the comfort and nurturing that my parents had never given me. They did not take me in their arms to console me. I was left alone in my grief and my sorrow for having to leave the friends I had finally made.

The last person John called said to him, "Why don't you pick up the Blue Hill paper and see what it has in the rental section?"

The next day John pulled up in front of the bookstore in Blue Hill and said, "Why don't you go in and get the paper?"

Well, this was a Wednesday, and I knew it was published on Thursday. I was about to say something nasty about it being the end of the week for the paper, and I doubted anything in it would still be available. But then I heard this little voice in my head say *Leslie, just go in and get the paper*. I did, and we found the most perfect apartment!

It was a small one-bedroom apartment, with two other rooms, each having a large picture window overlooking the water. At sunset, everything turned a beautiful soft pink. Every day, a bald eagle flew right toward our window, turned, and landed in a tree across the road. We could walk to everything in the little town—there was even a hospital within walking distance. It truly was a dream come true for me. When we moved in and I was sitting on the couch watching a great blue heron fish across the way, I called my friends and started singing, "I'm in heaven!"

There was only one problem, and it turned out to be a big one. It leaked! We were on the second floor of a four-story building—an old building that had been built in 1830. The strange thing is the two apartments above us did not leak, but the ceiling in both our front rooms leaked right next to the big windows. We would call the owner—a man we never saw in the five years we lived there—

and he would say, "I'll send Mick over to look at it." Mick, who was the handyman, would come over, look at it, and that would be it.

After a while it stopped leaking as much, but we did not know why until the young couple above us was moving. They knocked on our door and asked if we wanted to come up and see why our apartment was not leaking as much as it had been. We went up—Mick had cut a hole in the wall under one of their big windows and had put a cup in the wall. He told the tenants to empty the cup when it rained. We all laughed, and I asked, "Do you think that will be in the new tenant's lease—that they have to empty the cup?"

A few months later the apartment above us was still empty. It was dark and pouring rain. All of a sudden, water started streaming in right next to where I was sitting on the couch. John was in the other room, and I yelled to him, "John, go upstairs and empty the cup!"

He did and then went up there every time it rained. When Mick was getting the apartment ready to rent again and was about to fix the hole in the wall, John suggested that he put a siphon in the cup and leave it in the wall. The siphon took the water outside the building. That worked for a while until there was a fire on the fourth floor. Our apartment sustained significant water damage, and we had to move out for about three months.

Again, the Universe was looking out for us because we had no idea where we would live for those three months. It was the beginning of summer, and all the rentals were sky-high. One of our friends invited us out to dinner and a couple we knew joined us at our table. When we told the Cunninghams what had happened, they graciously said, "Why don't you stay in our winter house? We are in our summer house until the fall."

Their winter house was in Blue Hill and was far lovelier than our apartment would ever be. We stayed there for those three months, and the Cunninghams would not even accept money for the electricity. It was a wonderful gift at a stressful time. John went to our apartment every few days to see the progress or lack of progress that was being made. One day one of the carpenters came to him and said, "Did you know about that cup in the wall?"

Unfortunately, when they put everything back together, they failed to replace the cup, and after we moved back in, we started having major problems. The water, again, started pouring in through the ceiling in both of the front rooms and then also started coming in around the large windows. After one particularly stormy night, I was inspired to write the following poem. It was true that when I was in the bedroom, I could not hear the ferocious storm that was beating against the windows. The rest of the poem was my imagination.

A House Divided

In my room I don't hear the rain
only a whisper of the wind.

In your room, rain slams against the windows.

It runs down the walls
fills buckets I must empty again and again.

Is there no end to this night's fury?

In my room, it is quiet.

There is no storm.

I go back and forth between the rooms
seeking the safety of one
lured by the danger of the other.

You charge through the water
holding the baby high.

In the classified section of the weekly paper, we found an apartment in Ellsworth. The population of Ellsworth at the time was between 7,000 and 8,000—so it was much larger than Blue Hill, which had a population of about 2,500. We were moving to the big city!

Our apartment was new with hardwood floors, two bedrooms, and a beautiful new front-loading washer and dryer in the large bathroom. We had been living in apartments with the washer and dryer in the basements. The basements of each place we had lived were filthy. To have a clean place in my own apartment to do the laundry was pure luxury for me. There were two apartments in the building and two businesses. Our landlords, a couple much younger than we, lived downstairs from us in the other apartment. They were always making snide comments about me having lead feet. One day I had had enough and said, "I am sorry I cannot fly. It is something I am not adept at—yet!"

I never liked living in Ellsworth like I had in Blue Hill, but John and I continued to have a nice life there. I was just not cognizant of the fact that I was living John's life, just as I had lived Jerry's life when I was married. I waited in a coffee shop when John was at his many rehearsals. He was in at least four different bands, some concert bands, some jazz bands. And of course, I went to all his performances. John and I were together almost all the time. There were very few things I did for myself. During my twenty-four years with John, I took care of him through five surgeries and prostate cancer. The last and most major thing was when he had heart failure and fell off the couch and suffered a head injury. He had to be medevacked from the hospital in Ellsworth to the hospital in Bangor, where he spent a week. When he left the hospital, John left with a pacemaker and a defibrillator implanted in his chest, and he was suffering the effects of his head injury. As often is the case, it took this extreme event for me to start questioning my life. I started going to a therapist because I needed help and support. She encouraged me to look at things about myself that were hard for me to face.

Chapter 10

Who Am I?

Where I had fallen down, so to speak, when it came to following my Soul's Purpose in this lifetime was in the taking care of my own needs. As I look back over my almost seventy-five years, I can see in relationship after relationship—with my parents, husband, partner, friends—I went along with what they wanted me to do, who they wanted me to be. How could I know who I was when I always let the other person define me? Even when they said something like, "Oh, you would never do that," I would not contradict them even when I knew it was not true. No one ever knew who I was—mainly because I never used my voice to tell them. I had grown up in a family where it was not safe to use my voice. By never using my voice all those years, I never had a chance to discover who I was. It was automatic for me to *not* speak up, and I never realized what being quiet was costing me. I never developed a sense of self. How could I when I was busy being who everyone else wanted me to be?

When I was married, I lived my husband's life. When I lived with John, I lived his life. If I had worked outside my home, I think I would have at least developed that part of me. Though, it's also more likely that I would have been the person those at work wanted me to be. I did not know any other way of being. All my relationships ended when I finally stepped out of the character they had created me to be and voiced something that went against their vision of who I was.

Of course, I picked friends and partners who did not want me to be authentic, and when I finally was, they became angry and that was the end of the relationship. It happened with my husband, my parents, and friend after friend. It often was as simple as my saying, "No, I cannot do that."

This is hard for even me to believe but one time a friendship ended when I said, "I am not sure I will be available to do that. Let me check and get back to you."

My "friend" slammed down the phone, and that was the end of our relationship. She had been so accustomed to having me always agree to be available, that all I had to do was to say "maybe I won't be" and she became angry enough to end our friendship.

John and I had a nice relationship, but I felt as if I was dying inside. I felt that if I did not find out who I was, I was going to end up like a shriveled raisin, lying in the corner of a dusty room. That is the image I had. My therapist helped me see I had options. Because John had recovered from his heart failure and head injury and was now doing well, both mentally and physically, I realized I did not have to stay with him. I could leave, and I did, even though it was one of the hardest things I have ever done. When I left my husband, I was leaving an abusive relationship. When I left John, I was leaving a loving man, a man I loved and who loved me. I cried every day as I prepared to leave.

John would say to me, "You don't have to go."

And as tears streamed down my face, I would reply, "Yes, I do."

I left John almost five years ago and moved here to Virginia where I have been living alone. When I arrived, I felt like an empty vessel. I have been slowly filling it ever since. It has been difficult for me to realize this about myself, but *Who Am I?* is the question. The answer has not come quickly.

Toward the end of my marriage with Jerry, I had the first of many spiritual experiences—at least the first I was aware of. I now realize I had to have had others throughout my life. I just did not recognize them for what they were. This one was so powerful I had to see it for what it was. Jerry and I were traveling on our way to Tennessee to visit his family. It was a two-day trip, and we were staying overnight in a motel. I got up to go to the bathroom without turning on a light. The bathroom was pitch black. These experiences are hard to describe. There really are no words to truly depict what happened, but the bathroom filled with the most powerful Love, and I heard, "Everything will be all right."

At the time, I took that to mean everything would be all right with our marriage, and I tried harder to make things work between us, but they did not. Everything got worse, and when we were getting a divorce, I thought, *Why would God say everything would be all right when obviously it was not?* It wasn't until years later that I realized God meant everything would be all right *with me.*

Sometime during the first year after I left Jerry, I was driving home one night, and my car broke down. This was before cell phones, and I walked up to a house and knocked on the door. A young woman let me come in to call AAA. They said it would be an hour before a tow truck could get to me. I went back and sat in the car to wait. I became afraid, thinking of what could happen to a woman stranded on the side of the road. All of a sudden, the car filled with that Love, and when it did, I gasped and said, "That is what I am forgetting. You are with me always." A short time later, a police officer (or was he an angel?) came and stayed with me until the tow truck arrived. I do not think it is a coincidence he came upon me that night. I can still feel the care with which he helped me get up into the truck.

When I was still with John, one thing I did do for myself was go for a Reiki session every week with a wonderful woman named Trudi. As she was finishing our first session, Trudi said, "You are whole, perfect, and complete just the way you are."

Interestingly, that made me feel angry, and I told her that is how it made me feel. Somehow, saying that endeared me to Trudi. She mentioned it often and would say that at that moment she knew I was authentic. During one session, she told me she had had an amazing Soul Reading and suggested I go have one. That is how I met Rosie, a woman I have come to call my Soul Healer.

I just now listened to the recording of that Soul Reading again, and I realize it would have been advantageous for me to listen to it more often. It reminded me of the things that I was to do in this lifetime and the things that stand in my way and keep me from doing them. Rosie called in her guides and my guides as she started the session. We sat very close facing each other. For a couple of minutes Rosie took my hands to connect us. Then she sat back and listened to what my guides wanted me to know. For as many lifetimes as she could see—more than she could count—I had been in service to others. In all those lifetimes I was the head of a large religious order—an Abbess or an Abbot for I was a man as often as I was a woman. I kept coming back over and over again, reliving the same life—a servant of God and a shepherd of His people because I wanted to become perfect at doing it.

This lifetime is to be a Healing Lifetime for me. I am to recover from thinking only of the needs of others and focus on my needs. When I was the head of those large religious orders, I was responsible for many other people and the growth of their souls. I was very good at putting my needs aside as I focused on the needs of those in my care. In those Orders, I had to follow the dogma of the church and be sure those I was leading did the same. This lifetime I am to ignore all dogma and instead discover and concentrate on who I am as a spiritual being. I am to discover what I believe, not what I have been told to believe. I have been very true to my soul's calling in this respect.

I grew up in the Presbyterian Church, and I remember even as a child being told things that did not seem true for me. For a few years when Jerry and I were married, we attended a Methodist Church. But after that I said I could no longer attend any church because what they were teaching did not feel right. I have always said I did not believe in organized religion. I did not believe God had these rules and regulations. I began to believe organized religion was created by men to control the masses. It is interesting to me that I could go from all those lifetimes following the dogma of the Catholic Church to not believing in any dogma in this lifetime. I have been reading *Conversations with God* by Neale Donald Walsch, and what God says confirms all I have believed in this lifetime.

I recently took the Enneagram test and found out I am a Nine. When I listened to the characteristics of a Nine I thought, *How did they get inside my head?* It was uncanny to me how much this description fit. I do not know if we carry these things from one lifetime to another but after listening to the recording of Rosie giving my Soul Reading, I realized that my being a Nine fit right in to my being the leader of all those large religious orders. The Nine is the Peacemaker. What I have always thought of as a character flaw is really my strength. I can see all sides of an issue, of an argument. Nines make wonderful mediators, and yet I thought there was something wrong with me because, "Yes, I see your side, and yes, I can see your side also."

Because Nines are Peacemakers, we often go along with what others want, totally ignoring what we want. Rosie told me repeatedly throughout my Soul Reading that I was hardwired to be that way, and I guess it should not surprise me or upset me that I have carried that way of being into this lifetime. There are a couple of other things I think I have brought with me from my other lives. One is that I have an extraordinary ability to remember names. How many people do you know who say, "I always remember names"? Usually the opposite is true. Remembering the names of all the people under my care would have been very important, and I am sure that is why I can do it now. Another thing is that I do not like the air on my skin—of course I was always covered up by a habit or a cassock. And I am very happy living with very few possessions—as long as I have my books, I am happy.

When I was still with John and living in Maine, I attended my first four-day Spiritual Retreat with Rosie. There were about ten other women attending. It was during this retreat that I was first introduced to Archangel Michael and his power. I was reading a book about Michael each night before I fell asleep.

We were in a beautiful rural setting, and a number of women had gone outside and then come right back in saying, "There is a swarm of small bees out there that kept getting in my face." One afternoon I was walking between the building where I was staying and the building where we were meeting, and that swarm of bees got in my face. I barely had the word Michael out of my mouth when the swarm just disappeared! Poof—it was gone!

During that same retreat we had an exercise where we were to meditate to Wayne Dyer and James Twyman's *I AM* CD. Then we were to write something. This is what I wrote. I have always said I did not actually write it—it was dictated to me, and I wrote it down as fast as I could. I have now learned this is what others call a "Spiritual Download."

I Am This I Am

What is the Universe asking me to remember?

It is asking me to remember

I am strong and powerful.

I am an Amazon woman as tall as the tallest redwood.

I am the knowledge of the world.

I am the whisper of the wind.

I am as unique as a snowflake.

I am the eye of the storm.

I am the sand beneath your feet.

I am the sunrise and the magenta sunset.

I am as cool and clear as a mountain stream.

I am as thunderous as the mightiest waterfall.

I am as tender as a new leaf in spring.

I am as loving as a mother with her newborn.

I am the drumbeat of ancient womanhood.

I am the sweet sound of a flute.

I am the bird that calls your name.

I am all that is, all that was, and all that will be.

I Am This I Am

Chapter 11

My Spiritual Journey

I did not realize when I left John in Maine that I was starting on a spiritual journey—although our whole life is a spiritual journey. But it was not until I was seventy years old that I realized or learned that to be connected to the spiritual world, *I* had to make the connection. Those in the spirit world were always there waiting— waiting for me to invite them in. A bolt of lightning did not light up the sky and suddenly I knew—it was a slow awakening. It was being with others who were seeking the spiritual path, it was reading books and listening to religious leaders, it was meditating, it was having a spiritual counselor, it was just being open to receive.

Intuitively, I knew I had to leave John and Maine and be alone to do this. Even though it was so difficult to leave John, I knew I had to go. Rosie was living in Virginia Beach, Virginia, in the winter and spending the summers in Maine. I contacted her to see if she had room in a workshop she was planning on giving in Virginia Beach. When she heard what I was planning on doing, she said, "Leslie, my guides tell me you need a four-day one-on-one workshop with me." It was truly a blessing and a wonderful gift I was given. It was an expense I had not expected when planning my move, but what I received was priceless.

When packing my car in Maine, I reached down to pick up an empty bin and the wind caught it and knocked me onto my bottom. One minute I was bending over, the next I was sitting stunned on the ground. I had had lower back pain for years and at the time was being treated by a chiropractor. After falling, I went to her one more time before I left and I also had a massage, but I had been injured far worse than I realized at the time. When I gingerly and with great emotional and physical pain got into the car in Maine, I did not know where I was going to live. I knew I would know it was the right place when I got there. I thought it would be somewhere between my daughter's home in Northern Virginia and Atlanta where my sister lived. A couple of days after being knocked over, I drove two ten-hour days to get to my daughter's in Northern Virginia. When I arrived, I was in extreme pain—pain beyond anything I had ever felt, even in childbirth. I called my sister Deborah and told her I did not think I could drive to Virginia Beach to meet with Rosie. Deborah, who has always been there for me said, "You have to meet with Rosie. I am going to fly up and drive you down. I can stay with Dad when you are with Rosie, and then we will continue south until you find the place you want to live."

My daughter, Kelly, decided I had to go to the emergency room to see if I had broken anything—so I spent my seventieth birthday sitting with Kelly in the hospital. I had not broken anything, but it was devastating to me when the doctor came in and told me all the things that are wrong with my spine.

When I arrived at Rosie's, I was completely depleted emotionally, physically, and spiritually. One of the first things Rosie said to me is, "You will be a new person in four days."

I cannot say I was a new person, but I was certainly on my way to becoming one. Rosie nurtured me, counseled me, and fed me delicious nutritional meals three times a day. While I was there, Rosie often used the phrase *Soul's Calling*. I asked her what a *Soul's Calling* is, and she told me it is something you know you have to do, or you will regret it for the rest of your life. I had had a *Soul's Calling*.

I had known if I did not leave John, no matter how hard it was to do, that I would regret it. It is so interesting how our souls know all there is to know, and we in our human form often do not have a clue. The first day I was there Rosie said to me, "In order to heal, you have to reunite with your father."

We each have a different memory of what my response was: My memory is that I said I had been thinking of doing that, and Rosie's memory is that I said, "No! No! No! I do not want to do that!"

Each time I thought about seeing my father again, I started crying. There was much crying in those four days. Rosie conferred with our spiritual guides, and they told her my father and I had been adversaries for five lifetimes. The last two we were in battle against each other. I really tricked my father by coming into this lifetime as his daughter—something he was not prepared for and did not know what to do about. Of course, this was on the soul level. I called my sister who was at my father's (my mother had died years before without my seeing or speaking to her for almost eighteen years) and told her I wanted to reunite with my father who was ninety-three at the time.

She told me that when she told him what I had said, he started crying and said he would very much like that to happen. My sister asked me if I wanted her to be there or if I wanted to meet my father alone. I did not hesitate—I knew we had to meet alone. The night before I was to meet my father, Rosie was all excited. As we were eating dinner she kept receiving and sending texts. She said to me, "Oh! I think it is going to happen!" But she would not tell me what *it* was, and I could not imagine what she was planning.

I said, "What are you going to do—have a band come marching down the street?"

Well, it was better than a band! At about eight o'clock, a great big man and his wife-to-be arrived, and I was introduced to Robert and Karen. Robert is an opera singer and a friend of Rosie's. She had asked him the day before if he would come by and sing me a lullaby. He later told me that his guides said to him it was not a lullaby he was to sing to me; instead, he was to sing an aria from the Italian opera *Simon Boccanegra*. That night as I sat on a couch with tears streaming down my face, Robert stood behind me with his hands on my shoulders. In his booming voice he sang the beautiful aria "Il Lacerato Spirito" as Karen sat across the room, weaving a protective energy cloak around me. As I wept, I could feel the aria in every cell of my body.

When he was finished singing the aria, he sang "The Impossible Dream" from *Man of La Mancha*. This was one of the most amazing experiences of my life. As Karen and Robert were leaving, Robert said to me, "Why don't you live here? Why go off and live somewhere where you do not know anyone?"

That night as I lay awake, I could not think of any reason why I should not live here except that I did not want to. I thought I wanted to live in a place I had never lived before. I had lived in the Virginia Beach area on and off since I was five years old.

The next day, I went to meet my father at his favorite restaurant. It was two o'clock in the afternoon, and the restaurant was empty except for my father. As I walked in the door, he was sitting at the bar drinking a glass of water. He stood up and said, "It's you," and we hugged.

He must have told the waitress that we were meeting after being apart for many years because she seated us in a section and then drew a curtain across the doorway saying, "I will give you some privacy."

It was a booth, and my father asked me, "Do you want to sit across from me or next to me?"

And I asked him what he wanted. He said that he wanted to sit next to me, and that is what we did—with me on the inside. I had already had lunch at Rosie's, so while my father ate a salad, I had a bowl of ice cream. Rosie said I should limit my first visit with my father to one hour. When I told my father that I thought we should meet for just an hour, he waved his hand in a dismissive gesture, but he honored my request, and we met for an hour. I did not have to worry about what to say because my father did all the talking—talking about himself and never asking me one question.

At one point he said, "You are lucky I am a very forgiving person, not like your mother. If you had come back when your mother was still alive, she would have shut the door in your face."

And I said, "Maybe that is why I never came back."

Later, my sister told me my father had told her, "Leslie does not look like what I remembered."

And my sister said to him, "I am sure you do not look like she remembered you looking either."

Of course we didn't—we were both twenty-six years older!

Since I had decided to stay and not continue on my trip south, I went and stayed with my father after I left Rosie. I went from not seeing my father for twenty-six years to living with him for six weeks. He was driving me around to apartment complexes as I looked for a place to live. One Friday, the two of us were in Norfolk for lunch, and after lunch we went to look at apartments in Pembroke Towers.

They had a one-bedroom apartment available with the most magnificent view. It looked down the Hague, which is a man-made waterway, across to the Elizabeth River, and over to the City of Norfolk. The only reviews of the building I could find online were written by people who said they had to move because their apartments were overrun by cockroaches. I asked a woman in the lobby if she had roaches in her apartment, and she told me that she was visiting her son. In a few minutes she brought her son downstairs to tell me he had never had a roach in his apartment. I asked another woman if she lived in the apartment building. When she replied, "Yes," I asked her if she had roaches in her apartment.

She looked incredulous and said, "I have never seen one roach while living here. Would you like to come up and see my apartment?"

The view was wonderful, and the people were even more so. I signed the lease right away and have been happy here ever since. Though I am sorry to say I have seen more than one roach! Old buildings in the South are going to have roaches. Those two people were just lucky they had never seen one. I ended up with only one bedroom, but the rooms are large, and I have an eighteen-foot balcony. The Elizabeth River is a busy river. I see tugboats (I had no idea there are so many types of tugboats), barges, Navy ships, tankers, sailboats, large yachts, and before COVID, cruise ships would dock in view of my apartment.

One day I saw a Staten Island Ferry going up to the shipyard, which I can see from my apartment, and then about four months later I happened to be looking out as, newly painted, it was leaving to go back to New York. At night, the view is magical with all the lights of the city and the tugboats going down the river lit like Christmas trees. I never tire of watching the day slowly turn into the night as the light softens, casting the buildings in a golden glow.

I feel so blessed to have had this place as my sanctuary, especially during the time of COVID-19. Instead of this magnificent view, I could be looking out at the side of another building. My apartment is furnished with a mishmash of things. Half of the things were given to me by people who no longer wanted them. I would think to myself—*I need a file cabinet*. And someone would say, "Leslie, do you need a file cabinet?" Consequently, I have two beautiful oak file cabinets—one double and one single—that I use as my end tables. I needed a bookshelf, and someone asked me if I wanted the

I Am the Whisper of the Wind

one they were going to discard. And it went on and on like that. I love looking around and thinking about how each piece was given to me—all I did was think that I needed it and there it was!

People were knocking at my door and offering to give me the exact thing I was thinking about. It was the Law of Attraction at work. This was in addition to the things my father did for me. He not only gave me a few things I needed, he also used his truck to pick up and deliver some furniture I had bought. A table I bought was missing a metal brace, and he came one day with his tools and put a new brace on it. My father had always been good at solving this kind of problem. By doing these things for me, we were beginning to reconnect after all those years of being estranged.

My father seemed very happy to have me back. He told me he had gone to see his minister and talked to her about me and my returning, and they had both cried. After that, he called me his Prodigal Daughter. He was good to me—including me in many of the things he did. I think he knew he could not treat me the way he had before I left. Interestingly, our story *was* similar to the story of the Prodigal Son in the Bible, because my brother was furious that I had come home and had been welcomed with open arms by my father.

My father was the ultimate gadabout. He went out to dinner every night, usually accompanied by his lady friend Shirley.

My mother had died six years earlier. She developed encephalitis after being bitten by a mosquito in Key West and was in a coma for eight days. Even though she had a medical directive that would have allowed her to die, my father insisted that everything be done to bring her back. According to my sister, when she came out of the coma, it was as if she had had a severe stroke. My father had wanted her to recover, but he wanted her to be the way she was before her illness. He was unable to cope with the fact that she was not. They had a hospital bed moved into the dining room and hired someone to come in every day to help, but that did not last long because my father was angry and mistreated my mother.

She was moved into a nursing home where Shirley's husband was dying. As their spouses lay dying, my father asked Shirley to go out with him. Shirley was not interested. My mother died a year before Shirley's husband died. Shirley told me my father must have been watching the obituaries because as soon as Bentley died, my father called her. They never lived together, but she became his constant companion, having dinner with him every night and traveling with him when he traveled. Although, unbeknownst to Shirley, my father had numerous other women he fit in between his times with her. When my mother died, he had these other women come to the house and take anything of my mother's that they wanted. When my sisters arrived, all my mother's nice things were gone. It was always more important to my father to impress people he hardly knew than it was for him to be a loving father to his children.

Not only did my father go out to dinner every night, but he also often went out to lunch and always to brunch on Sunday. His restaurant bills were between $2,500 and $3,500 a month. He was a member of the Chrysler Museum and went to all its openings. He had season tickets to everything that had season tickets. He was a member of many Navy organizations. He was one of the founding members of the Sugar Plum Bakery, which trains and employs handicapped adults. He had served in numerous capacities in his church. He was very beloved in the community, and everywhere we went people would tell us what a wonderful person he was. Yes, he was wonderful to all the people "out there," but in so many ways, he was not wonderful to his family. He was not always kind to Shirley and often physically pushed her out of his way.

One night Shirley asked me how he had treated my mother, and I told her, "The same way he treats you."

He fawned over young women in her presence, physically pushed her out of the way, told embarrassing lies to others in front of her, dismissed what she said with a wave of his hand. For years my mother talked to me about how she wanted to leave my father. I remember when they had been married for forty years, she said to me, "You don't even get that for murder."

After watching my father practically fondle a woman's breasts while saying sexually inappropriate things to her, I decided I had to start seeing a therapist again. My question to her was—*Am I handling my father's behavior in a healthy way or am I dissociating as I had always done in the past?* She told me that if I was questioning whether or not I was dissociating, then I was not. However, she did help me navigate my relationship with my father.

Who we were was never good enough for my father. My brother was a flight attendant, but my father told everyone he was a pilot. My sister Deborah had been a college basketball player. My father told people she had been in the Olympics. My mother was a docent at the National Portrait Gallery, but she became the curator. My father told the most outlandish stories to people. My mother's family had come over on the Mayflower. My father's name was Earl and he told people he was an English Earl. Of all the lies he told this one infuriated Shirley the most. She was from Liverpool, and she was so angry when she repeated the story to me that she was sputtering with rage.

My ex-husband was an oral maxillofacial surgeon. When I returned and my father introduced me to people, I could hear him whisper that I *had been* married to an oral maxillofacial surgeon. As if that had anything to do with me. The first thing he said when introducing me was that I was seventy years old. He did stop that when I told him it was not necessary for him to tell people my age. Of course, the lies he told often made for awkward conversations with people. It was sad because no matter how good things were, they were never good enough for my father.

He wanted everyone to think he was wealthy, so he gave money away to waitresses he liked and to the young woman who came and helped him in the house. He bought a car for one waitress and paid for dinners for strangers in restaurants. One night I went out to dinner with him. Shirley was there also, as was one of his few male friends, and a young woman who had been the judge at an art show we had attended. At one point during the evening, I looked over and my father had a big wad of money in his hand, and he was counting it to show this woman (whose name also happened to be Leslie) how much money he carried in his pocket. I turned to Shirley and asked, "What is he doing with all that money?"

Shirley answered, "Oh, you know how men are. They like to carry a lot of money around."

I said, "Do you mean to tell me he gets drunk every night and walks around with all that money in his pocket?"

Shirley's answer was priceless. She said, "Oh, Leslie, he doesn't walk around. He goes out and gets into his car."

That night, he told Leslie that he could get her any job she wanted in the art community. About a week later, Leslie called me and asked me to meet her for lunch. During lunch she told me she had called my father and left him a message. He had not returned her call. Leslie wanted to know what I thought she should do—should she continue to call him? I told her to forget about it because there was no way he could get her a job. He was always telling waiters and waitresses he could get them any job they wanted. As we were leaving the restaurant, I told Leslie I was going up to Maine that summer to visit some friends.

She said to me, "Why don't you buy a house up there?"

I said, "I don't have that kind of money."

And Leslie replied, "Well, have your father buy it for you."

I turned to her and said, "Leslie, my father does not have any money." When Leslie realized my father did not have any money and could not get her a job, we never heard from her again.

One night my father and I went out to dinner—one of the rare times it was just the two of us. I was spending a few nights with him because they were putting a new roof on my apartment building and many of the parking places were blocked off, which meant there would not be a parking place for me if I returned home late in the evening. While we were eating, I told my father my mother had come to me several times since I had returned. I knew I could say this to him because he often told me he felt my mother's spirit with him in the house. But when I said this to him, he immediately asked in a nasty voice, "Well, has she forgiven you?"

When I said, "Actually, she asked for my forgiveness," he started attacking me verbally, bringing up things from the past—even things that concerned my daughter.

This became an amazing spiritual experience. As my father attacked me, I was pulled toward the left to attack back, and I had much ammunition I could use. But Spirit was whispering in my right ear, "Don't go there. Stay here." Every time I was pulled toward the left, I heard, "Don't go there. Stay here."

A couple of times I said to my father, "We cannot go back." But he kept it up—attacking, attacking. Finally, I said in a firm voice, "Dad! I am here now, and I love you, and I am happy you are my father."

He immediately stopped his attack. I do not remember what else was said after that, but when we returned home, he offered me the last of the after-dinner drink he always had before going to bed. There was enough for only one person, and he gave it to me. I knew this was my father's peace offering. The next night, I did not go out with him, but when he returned home, he hugged me in a way he had never hugged me before. And when he was dying, he would look up at me and smile, and I realized we had healed all those years of being enemies. We had connected spiritually in a beautiful way.

When my father was dying, he told us exactly what he wanted for his funeral service, and he said he did not want the gathering after the service to be in the church. He wanted it to be at one of the fancy country clubs. He told us what foods he wanted served and of course he wanted an open bar. I asked him if he was a member of the club (knowing he wasn't) and he told me he could get in anywhere he wanted to—evidently, even when he was dead. However, he did not leave any money for us to pay for his fancy send off.

When he did die, all four of us decided (and this in itself was amazing because we are not close—in fact my brother absolutely hates my sister Melanie and me) we would *not* have a funeral service for him and certainly not a party at the country club. Because he was involved in so many military and community groups, we knew the church would be packed. My father was very charming and loving to everyone except his four children. We decided we would not subject ourselves to having all those people come up to us and tell us what a wonderful loving person he was when he had not been that way to us.

We were surprised at how many people cried when we told them he had died, even the printer at the print shop. The only people who did not cry were his four children. People started calling, wanting to know when the funeral would be, and we told them that the family had decided to have a private service. Then we had people calling wanting to know where and when the private service would be. Shirley asked me when the service would be, and I told her there would be no service. She became angry and asked me what my father would want. She became even angrier with me when I said, "My father is not here." I was a good friend to Shirley, but after my father died, she cut off all contact with me.

We have to realize when we are true to ourselves, there may be those who are going to criticize us for it. In fact, that is often the case. People want you to do what they want you to do. They want you to be who they want you to be. I feel I do not owe anyone an explanation for my wishes or my behavior, and I do not ask others to explain theirs. No one knew why we did not have a funeral service for our father because we did not give them a reason. We wanted to be true to ourselves without speaking ill of our father.

Chapter 12

Godwinks

When I was at Rosie's for those four days, she took me to the Glad Helpers Healing Prayer Group at Edgar Cayce's A.R.E. (Association for Research and Enlightenment). The A.R.E. was founded in 1931 by Edgar Cayce to help people change their lives for the better. At the A.R.E., one can study subjects ranging from holistic health to spirituality, intuition, and reincarnation. The Glad Helpers was a group formed by Edgar Cayce to study his writings and pray for those who ask for prayer. Today, people from all over the world send in requests for prayer. The meeting has a set agenda. In addition to the study and discussion of Cayce's writings, and the reading of the names of those requesting prayer, there is a period of hands-on healing.

Inge was a member and from the first time I attended I was struck by her presence. She is a lovely woman originally from Austria who has so much knowledge not only about the Cayce readings but also about all aspects of spirituality. I was in awe of her. One day, she did a hands-on healing for me.

After she was finished, she said, "We have been together in another lifetime. You were my Mother Superior."

When she said that to me, she put her head down as if in reverence of me. I thought, *I was your Mother Superior? How could that be?*

I do not know anything in this lifetime about the things you are so knowledgeable about.

I said, "No wonder I have loved you from the first time I saw you." And I *had* loved her. From that moment on, Inge treated me as if I was still her Mother Superior.

Inge has written a number of books. One afternoon, the Glad Helpers sponsored a book reading and signing for her. I was sitting across the room from her, directly in her line of sight. As she read a piece from her memoir, I wept. I wept, and I could not stop crying. She looked across to me as if she understood, and she told me afterward that my weeping had such an impact on her.

Shortly after this, Inge moved to Baltimore to be closer to her children. The last day she was at the Glad Helper meeting she took my hands in hers, and as I wept again, she said to me, "We must have been very close to each other."

Of course, she meant in that lifetime when we were together in the monastery. I had never questioned what Rosie told me during my Soul Reading—that for as many lifetimes as she could see I had been the head of a monastery—either as a Mother Superior or an Abbot. I did not question it because even though it was amazing to me to think of myself that way, it felt right. So many things about how I am in this lifetime make sense to me when I think about what my life would have been like living in a monastery. But having Inge say we had been together was amazing proof to me that Rosie had been right.

I do not have the ability to see past lives as Inge is able to—yet. I say *yet* because though some people are born with special abilities, others of us acquire them as we travel down the spiritual path. The more I have studied spiritual teachings, the more connected I have become to God, the angels, my teachers, and guides. I am able to hear their messages and often I can see an image in my mind. I know that in the past there were times I had a connection, but I ignored it, not realizing its significance. Now that I live immersed in spirituality, I see signs everywhere. I imagine they have always been there—I just did not see them—mainly, because I was not looking for them. Past incidents have taken a more profound meaning as I look at them through this new lens.

This experience I had in Maine is an example. In the summers, John and I would go to Bar Harbor on Sunday afternoons. We would sit on a hill overlooking the water. Then we would go to a funky coffee shop called the Internet Café. We would get a coffee and sit at one of the tables and play Scrabble. For a couple of weekends, a young couple from southern Maine would be there playing Scrabble also. We talked to them and learned he was in the military and was slated to go to Afghanistan in the fall. They were coming to Bar Harbor as often as they could on the weekends to enjoy their time together before he left. After seeing them one weekend, every time I thought about her, I would sob. I would sob with a terrible pain in my heart. I wondered, *Why am I sobbing about someone I do not even know?* That night I had a dream. I dreamed that I had finally found a woman I had been searching for for many lifetimes. In the dream, we had built a beautiful garden together. When I woke up that morning, I realized I had loved this woman in another lifetime, and I (my soul) had been searching for her, and I had found her at the Internet Café! I never saw her again, but after that dream, I was at peace whenever I thought about her. Thinking back on this, I now realize that even though I cannot see things the way Inge is able to, I have gotten messages through my dreams.

The Glad Helper meeting was the place where I was most spiritually nourished. I was with like-minded people who were seekers, who were people wanting to be connected to God and the Universe of Spiritual Beings—the Holy Spirit, angels, teachers and masters, Jesus, and Mother Mary. There is a wonderful book by SQuire Rushnell titled *When God Winks at You*. Rushnell explains that God shows us His love by the things we think of as coincidences, and Rushnell calls these "godwinks."

Well, one week God winked at me during the Glad Helper meeting. The meditation room where we met had a window that looked out across to the Atlantic Ocean. This particular day I was asking myself, why am I here? I was feeling unloved and wondering why I was here on this earth. As I looked out the window, I saw a red kite. I kept looking at the kite and thinking that it meant something, but I didn't know what it was.

That night, I opened a book I had bought on Amazon for my little grandson Oly's birthday. I had picked it out because I had given Oly a book for Christmas by the same author and illustrator, Nancy Tillman. Her books are beautiful books with beautiful messages. I had forgotten what the title was and when I opened the package, I was amazed to see the title, *You're Here for A Reason*. Then on the inside flap was a red kite! The kite appears throughout the book and the next to the last page says, "I just can't imagine a world without you." Followed by the last page: "You are loved."

At that moment, I had no doubt God loved me!

SQuire Rushnell's book became its very own godwink for my friend Kimberly. Kimberly and I are the dearest of friends even though she is the same age as my daughter. Kimberly lives here in Virginia, though this happened while I was living in Maine. Kimberly's daughter Taylor had cerebral palsy, and her health was deteriorating. Kimberly would often call me to tell me how Taylor was doing, and she and I would end up crying together over the phone. I decided I wanted to send her *When God Winks at You* because it is a comforting book, and I wanted her to know that God and I both loved her—and Taylor, too. Each of the stories shows how God orchestrates things to come together for people in the most amazing ways. I ordered the book from the bookstore in Bangor.

Usually, when I ordered a book from them, it would arrive in a couple of days. I wanted it sent to me so I could wrap it as a gift before sending it to Kimberly. This time the book didn't come, and it didn't come, and it didn't come. I called the store numerous times, and they would tell me they were trying to find a copy. The book finally arrived the week before Thanksgiving. When I mailed it, the woman at the post office told me it would not be delivered until after Thanksgiving.

The Saturday before Thanksgiving, Taylor's service dog started hemorrhaging and Kimberly rushed him to the vet. Sadly, Bodie had to be put to sleep. This was devastating for Kimberly, and she went home and told her husband Keith, "There is only one person I want to talk to, and it is Leslie, but her sister and Linda are arriving in Maine today to spend Thanksgiving with John and her, so I do not want to call her."

Shortly after Kimberly told Keith this, he went out to the mailbox and came back into the house saying, "Look what you got."

It was the package from me that was not supposed to arrive until after Thanksgiving, and there it was, arriving on the day Kimberly needed me the most! If it had not taken so long for me to receive it from the book store, it would not have arrived on that day. I believe these things are orchestrated by God to bring us comfort, and as SQuire Rushnell says—to show us God's love for us.

Having faith that God wants the best for me allows me to look at situations that would have been upsetting to me in the past. I know that with my limited view I cannot see or know what will come next. Recently, a man I was starting a relationship with walked out my door saying he would be right back. He never returned and did not answer my texts. I cannot say it did not hurt at the time, but the pain did not last long because I could imagine the Holy Spirit saying to me—*Leslie, he was not the right one. He had to leave so the right man could come in the door.*

How comforting it is to know that if I just let go and allow, God will make my life more magical than I can ever imagine. Now when something starts to upset me, I say, "Everything always works out for me." And it does! At the time I may not be able to see how it is going to work out, but I do not have to know. I trust that God knows. Saying this to myself keeps me in the positive mindset to receive what better thing God has in store for me.

In October 2018, I gave myself a gift of a week-long Women's Healing Retreat at the Outer Banks in North Carolina. It was in one of the big vacation homes across the street from the ocean. I had seen a notice about it at my counselor Pamela's office. When I read it, I knew it was something I was to do, and it turned out to be one of the most extraordinary weeks of my life! I did not know the women who were putting it on and I did not know any of the attendees. Even though I am definitely an introvert, I do not have any trouble going into situations where I do not know anyone. It may be because I have had to do it most of my life. I highly recommend stepping out of your comfort zone to do things. That is the way we invite miracles into our lives. There were about thirteen of us attending. I was the oldest one there and a few women were in their twenties. I thought how marvelous it was that they were exploring the spiritual world at such a young age. I was seventy before I started my exploration. The two women, Krista and Erika, who were putting on the retreat are both Shamans. They are good friends but could not be more different from each other. Krista is soft spoken, married and the mother of four children. She is traditional in her dress and manner, and I do not think she has any tattoos. Erika on the other hand is covered with tattoos and piercings. She has a childlike wonder about her. She gets excited and scrunches up her shoulders in delight. I immediately fell in love with Erika!

As we were sitting around visiting on the first evening of the Healing Retreat, Erika asked, "Does anyone have a relative named Billy who died when he was a young child?" Thinking about my mother's little brother who died when he was four or five, I said, "Yes." Then I realized his name was Robert not Billy. Erika said Billy had been on the Earth since he died, and that day she had helped him go to the Light. She described it in this way—An angel came down, turned into his mother and when he ran into her arms, she took him up to the Light. Erika said, "Now he is back to thank the person who brought him here, and he is walking around carrying a red balloon and saying, "Where is the carnival? I can't find the carnival."

In addition to all the exercises and Shamanic rituals we did that week, there were many other things offered to us. One of them was a Shamanic cleansing session. Even though I had no idea what that was, I decided to have one. I was the only one with my own bedroom. I was reading a novel before I went to sleep each night. It was on the floor, and I did the strangest thing before Erika came into my room for my cleansing. I thought—*I do not want Erika to see what I am reading.* So I put a notebook on top of the novel. After the cleansing, Erika and I sat in chairs and discussed what had happened. She said she had to write some things down, and she reached over and took the notebook I had placed on my novel. Then she told me more about "Billy." She said that he had not shown her his face until he turned to her and said, "It's not Billy. It's Bobby!" Of course Bobby is a nickname for Robert—my mother's brother. She said that Robert/Bobby had been with me my whole life because he was attracted to my Light. Before all of us had arrived on Sunday, Krista and Erika had walked through the house to check on everything, and when they entered the room where I was to stay, Erika said to Krista, "The person who is going to stay in this room is going to bring someone with her." And that "someone" was Robert's spirit. Unbeknownst to me, I had brought him with me as he had been with me my whole life. Erika did not remember saying this until she walked back into my room that day for the cleansing.

Erika again told me about Bobby walking around with his red balloon saying, "Where is the carnival? I can't find the carnival." During my healing, Jesus, Archangel Michael, and my mother were some of the spirits who were there with us. Erika said to me, "Your mother wants me to give you a gift. She wants me to give you this Miraculous Medal (a medal of the Virgin Mary) that a nun gave to me when she rescued me off the street when I was a child." Then she put it around my neck. I knew this must be a very precious thing to Erika and I said, "Why would you listen to my mother?" Erika answered, "Because an angel was standing next to her." I have worn it constantly since Erika put it on me but when I first started wearing it, I wore it under my clothes. One day the thought came to me— *You are supposed to wear this so everyone can see it.* And that is what I do now. As we were leaving the room that day Erika looked down and because she had taken the notebook off of the novel, she could see what I was reading, and she said, "Oh my God, Leslie, look at what you are reading." The title of the book was *Don't Stop The Carnival*! Each word was printed in a different color, and the word carnival was printed in red. That is why Bobby was looking for the carnival with his red balloon—he was looking for me! I believe Spirit told me to cover the book so Erika would tell me the story before she saw the title. Covering the book was truly a strange thing for me to have done.

Chapter 13

Lessons from My Daughter

Mother-daughter relationships can be fraught with landmines, torpedoes, and IEDs. While I have loved and adored Kelly and did my best as a mother, this relationship is the most painful I have experienced. My daughter is the person who taught me that one's heart can truly be broken. There were times in my life when I thought my heart had been broken, but those were just dress rehearsals. At the same time, this is the relationship that has allowed me to learn how to love myself and attain a true sense of peace.

Kelly was an adorable baby and child who grew into a beautiful woman. She is smart and capable and very, very funny. I wanted so much to be a better mother to her than my mother had been to me, but we can only give what has been given to us. My wonderful psychiatrist, Dr. P, explained it to me this way—we are like computers, and we can operate only with what has been put into us. It was he who helped me heal my broken parts, but by this time Kelly was a grown woman and the patterns in our relationship were already in place.

Kelly and her husband Roger met their freshman year at James Madison University in Harrisonburg, Virginia. This was long before cell phones or even portable phones. So instead of talking every day, Kelly and I talked about once a week. She always mentioned this boy named Roger. He was part of the group of friends Kelly did things with. Kelly said he wanted to be more than a friend, but she was not interested. She kept trying to set him up with each of her single girlfriends, but he had eyes only for Kelly. At the very end of their first year, during our weekly phone call, Kelly casually mentioned going out with Roger. I said, "Wait a minute. Did you say you went out with Roger, the Roger you have spent all year telling me you were not interested in?"

"Yes," said Kelly. "I asked myself why I had been waiting for Mr. GQ to arrive when I had this man who was treating me like a queen."

"Kelly," I said, "there are many women who go through their whole lives without figuring that out."

Kelly and Roger married in October 1990, ten months after I had left her father. I was living in Virginia Beach, Virginia, and Kelly and Roger were living four hours away in Gaithersburg, Maryland.

They bought a condo and adopted a cat soon after they married. When we sat down to our first dinner together in their new condo, the cat, Shelby, promptly jumped up onto the table and walked across my placemat. For some reason Kelly felt I should love her cat as much as she did, but not being an animal lover to begin with and having her walk across my placemat did not endear Shelby to me. That was strike number one.

That night I sneaked into the kitchen in the dark to fix myself a glass of Metamucil before going to bed. Kelly and Roger had already retired for the night, and Kelly came running into the kitchen from their bedroom hissing at me that I was making too much noise because the spoon was hitting the glass. Strike number two.

I do not remember strike number three, but I am sure there were at least three strikes against me before I left to go home from my first visit with them as a married couple.

Kelly and Roger had my first grandchild, Lily, in February 1995. They were living in their new house in Germantown, Maryland. John and I drove up to help Kelly celebrate her twenty-eighth birthday on the fifteenth. Lily was born on the eighteenth. I was in the delivery room when she was born, and it was the most amazing experience. When I arrived at the hospital and stepped into the elevator to go up to the delivery room, a handsome young doctor got onto the elevator with me. We realized as we talked that we were both going up to see the same mother deliver her baby—I was her mother, and he was her doctor. I held Lily when she was just minutes old. I looked into her eyes as she looked into mine. It was a beautiful moment. I was a grandmother at age forty-eight.

Since I was not working, I was able to help Kelly whenever she needed me. Before Lily was a year old, they moved to California for eighteen months for Roger's job. I flew out to California once while they were living there. Kelly had taken thousands of pictures of her firstborn, and she called me to come out and help her organize them. One afternoon, I was taking care of Lily when Kelly and Roger went out to do some shopping. Lily was walking by this time. She went into the pantry where the cat litter box was. I put my fingers out and she grabbed onto them. I was gently lifting her up to take her out of the pantry, and her elbow dislocated. The strikes were quickly mounting.

This was still the time before cell phones, so I sat with Lily with her arm tucked into mine until her parents came home. When Kelly called Lily's pediatrician, she said, "Oh, bring her into the office. This happens all the time with children, and we have someone here who can just slip it back into place."

Thank goodness I was not arrested for child abuse! Would you believe I did it again to Lily's sister, my second granddaughter, Isabel, who was born in 1997? How many grandmothers can say they dislocated the elbows of two of their grandchildren? It certainly is not something to be proud of. It was very bizarre with

Isabel as I think it was with Lily. Isabel was crawling around my feet, and when I picked her up, I did not realize she was holding my shoelace. When I gently lifted her up, it dislocated her elbow. I cringe now when I see parents swinging their children around by their arms. Their little joints are not meant to hold all their weight.

When they returned from California, Roger's job required him to work on projects in different cities. He would be gone all week and would fly home for the weekend. Every couple of months, I would go up to Germantown and stay with Kelly, Lily, and Isabel. I usually stayed for ten days to two weeks. Many times, I never left the house the whole time I was there. I cooked, cleaned up the kitchen, did the mending, took care of the children when Kelly went out, and at night, crawled around on the family room floor picking up the toys so that when Kelly got up in the morning, everything would look neat and tidy.

At Christmas time I wrapped all her presents—even my own. I baked dozens and dozens of muffins for her to give neighbors, the school bus drivers, and the teachers. One night when I was sitting in bed reading, Kelly came in, sat on the bed, and said, "Roger and I would like to buy a long-term health insurance policy for you."

I said, "Oh, Kelly that is so expensive. Thank you, but don't do that."

Her answer was, "MOM, when the children are grown, Roger and I are going to want to travel and do things. We do not want to have to be thinking about you!"

I thought but did not say, *I wouldn't want you to have to think about me either, even if I have to die all alone in a little closet.* They did not buy the insurance, but this was a foreshadowing of the things to come. Looking back, I believe I was trying to make up for everything I had done wrong when Kelly was a child. But evidently, I could not compensate for past transgressions, and I kept piling up new ones all the time.

When Lily was five and Isabel was three, Kelly was pregnant with their brother. Thanksgiving of 2000, Kelly invited John and me to come and help them celebrate the holiday. This was the first and only time we had been invited to spend a holiday with them. We were still living in Norfolk, Virginia, and we drove up for the weekend. When we arrived, Kelly informed me, not asked me, that John and I were going to take care of the girls on Saturday so she and Roger could go Christmas shopping. We celebrated on Friday instead of Thursday so that on Thursday, I could help Kelly bake the pies and get other things ready for the big day. While preparing the dinner, I was mashing the potatoes with a handheld mixer. I lifted the mixer out of the bowl while it was still running, throwing potatoes all over the kitchen. Kelly was infuriated with me. I felt as I did as a child, afraid to move because making a mistake invited the wrath of my parents. And for some reason I always made at least one big mistake while visiting Kelly—maybe because I was so afraid of doing so.

After that fiasco, we got dinner on the table and ate. We left the dishes and the eating of the pie until after we got home from driving through the nearby state park to see its beautiful Christmas light display. As we drove through the park, John and I were sitting in the very back of the van, and we occasionally commented on the display. Every time we said something, Lily told us to "Shut up!"

After exiting the park, Roger pulled over, got out of the van and opened the door next to where Lily was sitting. He was furious. We could not see what happened, but when he got back into the driver's seat, he said to Kelly, "Lily socked me and gave me a bloody nose!"

After arriving back home, we sat down to have dessert. Isabel was sitting on Kelly's lap, and she deeply scratched Kelly's cheek from just under her eye down to her chin. Kelly screamed. Roger jumped up, snatched Isabel off Kelly's lap and whisked her out of the room for a few minutes. That was it. Neither girl was in any way disciplined for their behavior.

While I was doing the dishes, I said to Kelly, "So how long is our duty tomorrow?" meaning how long were we going to be taking care of the girls. Now the word *duty* is a military term. I had spent my first forty-four years connected to the Navy, first with my father and then with my husband. We would often call something the "*dirty duty*" but that night I used just the word *duty*. However, that was bad enough because Kelly became enraged.

She got up in my face, as the saying goes, and started yelling at me about what a terrible mother I was, how when I came all I did was sit with my feet up and do crossword puzzles. She ranted and raged and went on and on. I was shocked. It was so far from the truth of what I did each time I came. Evidently, at one time, I had told Kelly that I would always be there for her. According to what she said that night, I had committed a grave injustice when I had recently told her I could not drive the five hours to take care of the girls (I had something else I had to do) when Kelly went to Parents' Night at Lily's school.

For some reason in all of this I said, "Kelly, the girls both hurt you and Roger tonight and nothing was done about it."

At that, Kelly snarled at me that if I did not approve of the way she and Roger were raising the girls, I was not welcome to ever come back. As I stood there with tears running down my cheeks, I said, "John and I will leave tomorrow morning."

The next morning when I was packing to leave, Roger, who is the peacemaker, came downstairs and said, "Leslie, don't leave. Kelly just wants you to be happy to take care of the girls. She doesn't want you to think of it as a difficult chore."

I said, "Roger, it is hard taking care of two little children. You know that."

We did not leave. We stayed, but even after all these years, it is extremely painful for me to think about what happened.

What I did not know at the time is that Kelly had many more arrows in her quiver. After we returned home, Kelly and I did not speak until Cameron was born in April. Because of our estrangement, Kelly asked her mother-in-law, Elynor, who lived close to them to take care of the girls when she and Roger went to the hospital. Just after Cameron was born, Kelly called me and said, "Mom, can you come help me? Elynor is not capable of doing it."

Of course, I went.

I had been waiting for Kelly to call and apologize. It never happened. But when she needed my help, I was there for her. Years later when Kelly and I were talking on the phone, the Thanksgiving massacre was mentioned, and I said to Kelly, "I was wounded by your words, and you never apologized."

Kelly's answer was, "MOM! I was pregnant!"

And I thought, *but you are not pregnant now*. Maybe, if I had been able to use my voice and say something in return, our relationship would have had a chance to heal. I don't know. Because she has talked to my sister, I know she holds things against me from her childhood—things I cannot go back and fix. But one important thing I learned is I could not make up for the past by what I did in the present. Never again, when I visited, did I work as I had done. I would help of course but nowhere to the extent that I did before she blew up at me that Thanksgiving.

I was not a mother who told her daughter what to do and how to do it. There was only one time I gave any advice to Kelly, and it was because she had asked me for it. When Isabel was born, Lily's behavior changed dramatically. Overnight, she went from being an enjoyable child to being a terror. Kelly asked me what she could do. I said, "Kelly, Lily needs to know you are the boss. She will constantly try to be in control, but for her to feel safe, she needs to know you are in control."

Kelly did not like my advice, and never asked for it again. When her pediatrician told her the same thing, she changed pediatricians!

I do want to stress that Kelly and I did have times when we enjoyed each other. We did not go out and do things together, but after the children were in bed each night, we would sit, talk, laugh, and eat some delicious dessert. We both have a good sense of humor, and Kelly is a wonderful storyteller and mimic. But for me, there was always the feeling I was being judged. I was. And I constantly came up short.

What Kelly and Roger did not know at the time of Cameron's birth was that Roger's mother was in the early stage of Alzheimer's. As it became apparent that she could not live on her own, they moved her from her condo to an assisted living facility. The facility assured Roger and his brother and sister they were the right facility for Elynor, and she would be well taken care of there. Unfortunately, they were not able to provide the level of care that Elynor needed as her Alzheimer's progressed, so the family had to move her again. Eventually, the family had to hire someone to be with her during the day.

Throughout this time, even when Elynor was in the advanced stages, Kelly was extremely loving to her, always patient and kind. When Kelly and Roger first married and when Lily was born, Elynor said many very hateful things to Kelly. Kelly once told Roger that the only good thing about Elynor having Alzheimer's was that Elynor forgot how much she disliked her. Kelly cared for Elynor by taking her to her many doctors' appointments, by being sure she had everything she needed, by visiting her and taking the children to see her, and by being sure she was included in all the family celebrations. I was actually surprised by Kelly's devotion to her mother-in-law, a woman who had at one time gone out of her way to be mean to Kelly. As I watched her with Elynor when I was there on my October visits, and when I heard from Kelly about what she was doing for Elynor, I thought—*Maybe there is hope for me.* But I was wrong.

One year when I was getting ready to leave to go back to Maine, Kelly asked me to help her with her knitting. There was a chair in the family room where we could sit together. As I sat there with her, I had the most intense desire to take her in my arms and tell her I loved her. I did not do it. I left, and for two years, every time I thought about it, I cried, cried because I had not acted on my desire. Two years later during another visit, we were standing in her kitchen. We were facing each other, and I started crying.

"Kelly," I said, "I want to tell you something."

As I stood with tears streaming down my face, I told her about what I had wanted to do and how I had cried ever since for not doing it. She stood with her arms by her side and as her mother wept, she said in a monotone, "Thank you for telling me that. I have always wondered."

It was at that moment I realized why I had resisted the impulse to take her in my arms. Somewhere inside of me I knew that is how my love would be received.

While there for my October visit during Lily's first year at the College of William & Mary, Kelly and I drove down to spend the day with Lily. I had known Kelly had had a big party for Lily when she graduated from high school. I had not been invited, but while sitting in Lily's dorm room, I realized her grandfather, my ex-husband, had been invited. Lily's bulletin board was covered with messages from all the people who had attended. As I sat reading them, I saw the one from Jerry. That is when my heart truly broke, and all I wanted to do was go home. I had planned to go from Kelly's to my sister's in Atlanta, but I called Deborah and told her I was going back to Maine instead. I gave her the excuse that I was worried about the economy crashing.

For years, my sister would mention the time I gave her that crazy excuse for why I was not coming to see her. Finally, I said, "Deborah, that is not why I did not come." Then I told her the real reason.

She said to me, "Why did you not tell me, your own sister?"

I replied that my heart was so broken I could not even talk about it. I never said anything to Kelly about it.

I continued visiting every October, timing my visit so I could take care of the children for a weekend while Kelly and Roger went away to celebrate their anniversary.

I arrived for my October visit with bags of wrapped Christmas presents for them to put under their tree in December. Maine has so many beautiful little stores and art galleries, so all year I had fun searching for and finding unique gifts for the family. Each year I gave the girls an angel tree ornament and Cameron, a Santa.

One year during my visit, I said to Kelly, "Maybe when the children grow up they will have a little Mimi (what they called me) tree with all the ornaments I have given them." Kelly's answer was a derisive laugh just like the one her father always used when I said something to him.

There is no mistaking that Kelly does not want anything to do with me. A strange thing is she sends me gifts and cards for each holiday. However, I have not seen her or spoken to her in five years even though we live only four hours apart. She does not text me except a short generic greeting on holidays. When my father died, she texted me saying, "I am sorry to hear about your father."

I have sent her many notes telling her how much I love her, and what a wonderful person and mother I think she is. In one note I told her that if she wants to tell me why she is angry, I am here for her. I ended the note by saying, "I love you—remember that."

I have not received an answer to any of them. By excluding me from her life, Kelly has essentially cut me out of the lives of my grandchildren. My granddaughter was married in November of 2022, and I was not invited as I have not been invited to any other of their celebrations. I live only hours away from them, and I am alone. Kelly's children are adults now, but they must know how she feels about me, and they would never go against their mother. She is by far the dominant one in the family. What is Kelly holding against me? I do not know. Is it something I did recently or something from her childhood? Whatever it is, I would love to have the opportunity to heal our relationship, but I cannot do it alone. Kelly must also want us to heal.

Thanksgiving of 2021, Kelly sent me a text telling me that they were all together for the holiday and having a wonderful time. She sent me this hurtful text when I was home alone not having been invited again.

The next year right after Isabel had been married, I decided to send Kelly a text before she had the chance to send me another unkind text. In it, I wished all of them a Happy Thanksgiving and said, "Even though you do not include me in your family, I hold all of you in my heart and love all of you dearly."

She did not answer, and I have not heard from her since. No more cards or gifts or texts. She has closed the door, completely cutting me out of her life. She is close to her father who was so nasty to her during her teen years. When we were still speaking, she would call me to tell me when her father would be visiting so I would not call during that time. I once asked, "Is he still married to Vicki?"

Kelly replied, "Oh no, Mom. That marriage lasted only a year. Every time he comes now, he brings a different young woman, very young, often younger than I."

All I could say was, "Kelly, I am so sorry."

This year, 2023, I decided to send my granddaughters each a text a week before Thanksgiving. I was tired of being silent and acting like having no relationship with my family was normal and okay with me.

To Lily I wrote: "Lily, maybe next week when you are all gathered together thinking of what you are grateful for, you will take a moment to remember your Mimi who was there at your birth, who held you and looked into your eyes moments after you were born, who was your 'Mimi Coat' when you were cold, who sent you a note every week when you were away at school, who has been robbed of years of your life for who knows why. I don't. Do you? But who thinks of you always and loves you dearly. Mimi"

To Isabel I wrote: "Isabel, maybe next week when you are all gathered around thinking about what you are grateful for, you will remember your Mimi who has loved you from the moment you were born, who felt such joy when she was with you, who took you to your art class when you were just a tiny girl. I remember walking through the parking lot, holding your hand and teaching you to watch for the back-up lights on the cars. Who has always celebrated you and your many accomplishments—even though I was not allowed to be there. Who has been robbed of years of your life for who knows why. I don't. Do you? Know that I think of you always and love you dearly. Mimi"

I did not receive a response from either of them. And so again I was alone while they all were gathered together, celebrating the holiday.

I was raised by a mother who *could not* love me, and I have a daughter who appears not to love me either, and grandchildren who are apparently following in their mother's and their grandmother's footsteps. The thing is, all I want to do is give love, to give love to everyone—the cashier at the grocery store, the homeless man on the street corner, the girl on the elevator, and my precious daughter, her husband, and children. I know nothing will be gained by my trying to figure out what I have done wrong. I believe I have never lived up to Kelly's expectations of me. She has judged me and found me lacking. And despite all of my efforts, I am not the mother she would like to have had. How happy can she be with all that anger locked inside? All I can do is send her my love whenever I think about her. I never discount the chance for a miracle. I know miracles happen all the time. I hold it in my heart that a miracle will occur, and Kelly will come back to me. The thing we have to remember with our children is that it is their journey and no matter what we may do that injures, hurts, or affronts them, it's still their journey. It is for them to work through it. We can apologize and take responsibility for our actions, but it is still their journey. We cannot travel their journey for them.

I realized after the Thanksgiving debacle and the five-month estrangement from Kelly that I had been wrong. I was spending all that time concentrating on Kelly and her family. Where was I in all this? I had been giving myself and my power away. I know now I was trying to make up for all the times during her childhood I had not been available to her because of my depression, but even after all these years she has not been able to forgive me. I wish I could say that I learned from this how to take care of myself, but all I did was switch my attention from Kelly to my partner John. It was not until I left John and started living alone that I began to concentrate on learning who *I am*. I did not know who I was. How could I?

For the last six years I have been acquainting myself with myself— not reacquainting, for I never knew. It has been a profoundly enlightening journey. I have learned that someone else cannot fill the hole we may have inside us—even the person who caused it. We can only do that for ourselves. It is definitely an inside job.

The same holds true for my son John. I have not written much about John. This is because I really do not know him. He left home when he was nineteen, and now he is in his early fifties. In all that time, I have seen him only three times, and talked to him only a few times on the phone. As I mentioned earlier in the book, when he first left home, he moved to Colorado to live with my brother and his wife. After living with them for a few years, he moved to the West Coast.

I rarely hear from him. He had a son when he was forty-eight. Although he and his son's mother are no longer together, they live on the same street and seem to be co-parenting in a beautiful way. I have not met my grandson, but John texts me more often now that he has a son. He sends me pictures of Oly and tells me things about him. Here is a poem I wrote about John while I was still in Maine. This was written over ten years ago, and since then I have seen John only once for a very short time about six years ago.

My Son

It has been thirteen years.

Would I recognize you
if I saw you on the street
or would I walk away?

Your sister tells me to go to a movie.

The actor looks exactly like you, she says
mannerisms and all.

I go.

Is that really what you look like?

Are you that handsome?

I might recognize you if I see you now.

But I won't know who you are.

Recently, someone asked me how I stay uplifted, how I stay connected to Spirit when life happens, when people do hurtful things, when they do not want to receive my love, or they laugh at me for who I am. I had to think about this for a while and then I had a wonderful realization. I have learned to love myself—to love myself deeply. And by loving myself and knowing I am totally and unconditionally loved by the Universe, other people cannot harm me. How could they? If what they do or say does affect me, it does not last long.

Years ago, one unkind word would stay with me for days, weeks, or even months. I would feel it physically as a stab in my chest, and I would not be able to stop thinking about it. I was hurt over and over again by that one unkind word. No longer does that happen. If something does bother me, I give it to the Holy Spirit and ask the Holy Spirit to take care of it for me. I have to confess that sometimes I keep taking it back from the Holy Spirit and then I have to return it. When I do that, I laugh and say, "Okay, Holy Spirit, here it is again."

One of the most healing things for me has been for me to connect with myself. I am my own best friend. I enjoy myself and my own company. I am constantly laughing at myself in a loving way. I laugh at my foibles and embrace my idiosyncrasies. I have given up trying to be perfect. I forgive my imperfections, knowing they are what make me who I am. I still have mean, unkind thoughts, but now after having one, I stop and say to myself, "I am sorry." I do this to remind myself that this is not the way I want to show up in the world. I have learned to not take myself seriously—to lighten up. Those old tapes in my head that shamed me and criticized me have gone the way of cassette players—they no longer exist.

Old hurtful memories do sneak in from time to time, but when they do, I can easily replace them with a pleasant, grateful, loving thought. This change—learning to love myself, forgiving myself, and being able to banish my negative thoughts—took years of practice, and I am still working on it. I have been very determined to change. My old way of thinking about myself was deeply ingrained and had been from early childhood, which is not something that magically disappears. It takes a very conscious effort. Because I no longer find fault with myself, what other people might think of me does not affect me in the way it once did. And because I am loving and kind and expect to meet loving and kind people, I do. I meet them everywhere. If I do come in contact with an unkind person, I know it has nothing to do with me.

My relationship to those in the spirit world is a casual relationship. There are no formalities. I do not have to do things to stay connected to Spirit. I am constantly connected. I do not pray a certain way. When I first wake up in the morning, I lie in bed and sing "Good Morning" to the angels and all the other heavenly spirits. I sing to my ancestors, my friends, and my family. As I name each one of them, I picture them with love in my heart. This is the most wonderful way to start the day. It opens my heart and fills me with love. All day I have spontaneous conversations with the wonderful loving spirits who constantly surround me. If I ask a question, I always get an answer. The other night I asked the angels what I should say to someone. When I heard nothing, I realized that was the answer—*do not say anything.* So I did not.

Recently, a friend gave me the book *Contacting Your Spirit Guide* by Sylvia Browne. In it, she says we have the same spirit guide by our side all our lives. I did not know this, although there have been times I felt his presence. She also said we can ask our spirit guide their name. I asked, and I immediately heard in my mind—Eric. I thought, *Really?*

So, I said, "If your name is Eric, you will have to show me proof."

The next day, as I was scrolling through the news on my phone, I saw Eric Trump. That still was not enough for me. That night, I said, "You are going to have to show me in such a definite way that I will have no doubt that your name is Eric."

I live in a high-rise apartment building, and the next day after saying this, I was on the elevator with my friend Ann.

She said, "The pest-control man, *ERIC*, is coming tomorrow."

The next day on the phone, Ann said, "The pest-control man, *ERIC*, came."

She has had the pest-control man come to her apartment many times, and she had never before used his name. And both times, she not only used it, but she also stressed it—as if she had been given a message to give me a message!

The following day, I went to the hospital to get an MRI. The woman who checked me in was named Erica. I finally said, "Eric, I hear you! Your name is Eric."

I have for many years felt the presence of my spirit guide. I did feel it was a masculine energy, but now knowing his name has made me feel so much closer to him, so much more connected. Now, I am constantly talking to him, something I did not do before knowing his name.

Another thing I have learned that makes life so much easier is I no longer expect people to be what I think they *should* be. It is a worthless endeavor to wonder why others act the way they do. We are each as unique as our fingerprints. We are here to remember who *we* are.

Although we may not always show it, we are love and we are here to love and forgive ourselves and others. This is the main reason we are here. What could we learn if we all were the same, if we all acted the same and liked and disliked the same things? Every experience we have and every person we meet gives us an opportunity to grow spiritually. I want to be an example of love, an example of forgiveness, an example of peace and grace and serenity. So, to answer my friend's question—by living this way, I am able to stay connected to Spirit when life happens.

Chapter 14

Angels Everywhere

In addition to spirit guides, we each have a guardian angel who is with us always. Our guardian angel is connected to our soul throughout all our lifetimes. I had always pictured my guardian angel to be a man dressed in an old-fashioned tweed suit. I pictured him to be a very serious, staid angel. One day I was reading that we can ask our guardian angel his or her name. I asked my angel what his name was, and she said, "Peggy."

I thought *What kind of name is Peggy for an angel?* Then I heard the song "Peggy Sue," and I envisioned my angel Peggy dancing and twirling and twirling and dancing. I laughed and thought that God had assigned a perfect angel to be my guardian angel. Because I am and have probably always been in every lifetime a very serious person, God gave me an angel to lighten me up. Recently, I realized I have neglected Peggy. I always talk to Archangel Michael and all the other angels surrounding me, but I do not talk to Peggy. I have asked her to forgive me, but I know she is probably saying to me that there is nothing to forgive. No angel ever judges or criticizes us for anything we do. They love us unconditionally as do all those in the spirit world.

Angels surround us and are waiting for us to ask for their help. The only time angels will step in and change the course of an action without our asking is when our life is in danger, and it is not our time to die. Sometimes they do things for us that would be impossible for us to do for ourselves. It is only in looking back that I realize *that* is exactly what happened one snowy day in Maine.

At the time I could not figure out what had occurred. Driving in Maine can be very treacherous. The roads, often with no shoulders, are narrow and full of potholes. When going around a curve, you never know what you might encounter on the other side—a moose, a deer, a raccoon, a skunk, or a slow-as-molasses porcupine lumbering across the road—or it may be someone pulling out of their driveway. There are boulders and trees right next to the road. At night it is pitch black unless there is a full moon. When you add ice and snow, it is a wonder anyone survives.

This day I was driving three women home from our weekly writing group meeting. There was ice and snow on the road and instead of a shoulder there was a ditch. There were two curves one after the other. As I rounded the first curve, I saw there was a tractor trailer coming in the other direction. It had not been able to make the curve and its cab was in my lane. There was no place for me to go, and no time for me to get there if there had been. Amazingly, I felt no fear and somehow, we suddenly found ourselves on the road on the other side of the truck.

In unison my friends said, "Wow, Leslie, you are some driver!"

I did not know what had happened, but I did know it was not I who had gotten us out of that very dangerous situation.

And I said, "No, it wasn't I who did that."

I now know the angels somehow transported my car through—or was it over?—the truck. I do not know how, but I do know I owe our lives to the angels who are always there to rescue us when we are in danger.

I cannot imagine my life without angels. Yet, for seventy years I lived without them. They were there, of course, but I never acknowledged them. Now I talk to them constantly and thank them whenever I have a good idea or am reminded to do something. All day I am thanking them just for being a part of my life. When I get into bed at night, I love to open my arms wide and say, "Oh! Thank you, angels, for all you have done for me today. Thank you! Thank you! Thank you!"

The angels were given to us to make our lives easier. They are standing by waiting for us to ask for help, but the operative word here is *ask*. We have to ask, and most people never ask. I often have people who know this tell me, "Oh, I forget to ask."

I no longer hesitate to call on them for assistance and because I am constantly connected to them, I often do not even have to ask. They know I am willing to accept their help and they immediately rush to my aid, unbidden. There is no task too large or too small for them. Sometimes there are things that happen to me that I can only explain as an angel intervention.

One day I had a terrible yeast infection. I was miserable and knew I had to see a doctor right away, but I also knew how difficult it was to get an appointment for the same day or sometimes even the same week or same month. So, what did I do? I asked the angels for help. When I called the doctor's office, the woman told me she could get me in that afternoon! Yet, when I arrived at the given time and gave my information to the woman at the check-in desk, she looked and looked at her computer and then said, "We do not have an appointment for you. You are not on the schedule."

I told her that I had called that morning and had been given an appointment.

"Well, who gave you the appointment?" she asked.

I almost always ask for the person's name, but this day I had failed to do so. I just stood there calmly as the woman picked up the phone and started calling around to find out who had given me the appointment. She could not find the person I had spoken to—of course not—it was the angel I had asked to help me, and she was no longer answering the phone!

The woman finally said, "Since you are here, we will work you in."

She was perplexed, but I did not enlighten her. As much as I love to tell people about angels, I was quiet that day. I think I knew this woman would not understand. It would be like the day I told my primary care doctor about something that had happened to me. As I was speaking, she was looking at me with the strangest expression on her face.

I said, "You do not believe this, do you?"

She said, "No, I am sorry, I don't."

I told her, "You don't have to be sorry. I know it is true."

When I said that, she asked me the name of my psychiatrist as she typed it into my record! There are just some people it is better not to tell.

The one thing I have trouble staying calm about is my computer. I am so technologically illiterate that when I have a problem and call for technical support, I cannot understand the computer jargon the person speaks. I tell them that I could be their grandmother. I ask them to be patient with me because I grew up at a time when we still had party lines. Then I ask, "Do you know what a party line is?"

Nine times out of ten, they do not. If you do not know and are interested—a party line is when you share a phone line with a neighbor or neighbors. When the phone rings, it only rings in your house. If you want to use the phone and your neighbor is using it, you hear them talking when you pick up your phone, and you have to wait for them to finish before you can use the phone. Unfortunately for our neighbors who shared our phone line, I was a teenager and was often talking on the phone. I could hear their exasperated sigh every time they picked up the phone to use it.

When calling for support, I had always heard you were safe if you were the one contacting the person, but if someone called you, it was more than likely a scammer. I needed help one day and Googled Apple support. I got the phone number from the site and called. I cannot remember what the problem was, but the man said he would have to get into my computer to take care of it. This is where my ignorance about computers got me into trouble. In my ignorance (and the fact that I become so extremely anxious when there is something wrong with my computer or I cannot figure out how to do something on it), I let him in, and when he was finished, he talked to me about buying protection for my computer. He had me send him a check using my scanner on my printer—of course, he had to walk me through that too because I had no idea how to do it.

About six months later the same man called me. I recognized his voice. He told me they had been monitoring my computer and had detected suspicious activity. I again let him into my computer, and he then talked me into buying more protection for something like ten years. I ended up paying him $2,500 altogether. Then on Christmas Eve I was having trouble again. I decided to call the Apple store at the nearby mall. I got the number—probably by Googling it. I called and this nice man answered. I told him what was wrong, and he started questioning me. I told him about what the other man had done and how much money I had paid him. This man said, "Oh, sweetheart, you have been scammed. Apple never charges anything for support unless you need a part."

I did not cry right away. But as he continued to talk to me, I started to cry and said, "It is not the money I am crying about—although, $2,500 was and is a lot of money for me to lose. I am crying because I let someone scam me." It felt like such a violation.

This man said, "Oh, there are so many scammers out there, and they are all very slick. We at Apple cannot keep up with them. As soon as we shut one down, five more pop up."

Then he said, "I don't know how you got this number for me. The only people who have this phone number are the technicians in the stores. When they run into a problem, they call me. I am the Head of Technical Support for Apple."

This wonderful man the angels obviously connected me with said, "I would like to go into your computer to see if that other man left something in there, but I hesitate to do so because the last person to do it scammed you." I told him I was going to trust him.

He spent a lot of time checking everything in my computer and said nothing had been done to my computer—they were obviously just after my money. He told me to never use Google for phone numbers or official sites. The scammers create sites that appear to be official. Then he gave me his cell phone number so I could call him any time I had a problem. It was an expensive lesson, but I did not focus on the money I had lost. I focused on how wonderful it was that on Christmas Eve the angels connected me to an Earth Angel that was loving, kind, caring, and concerned. It made me realize how very much I am supported by the Universe. I am sure that if I had talked to the angels at the very beginning, this never would have happened.

As I have worked on this book, I have learned to ask the angels for help when I run into computer problems. I cannot tell how many times the book has disappeared as I was working on it. Needless to say, that is an extremely upsetting occurrence! Many times I do not have any idea on how to remedy the problem, but I am amazed when suddenly the solution is right there in front of me. Recently, a friend asked me when I was going to stop being amazed when the angels answer my request. I told her I hope I never stop being amazed. I am so very grateful for all the help they give me in every aspect of my life.

Angels, Angels Everywhere

You ask—If I cannot see them, are they really there?

Yes, I tell you—They are everywhere.

There are angels in the prisons
on the boardwalk by the sea.

They are there for each and everyone of us
wherever we may be.

The hospitals are full of them.

The battlegrounds are too.

They are always there waiting
saying—What can we do?

They wonder why it is so hard
for us to love each other
when God created us to be
each other's loving brother.

I wonder—

Would the world be a different place
if each of us saw the other
as having an angel's face?

Chapter 15

Emissary for God

I believe we are all here as emissaries for God. We are not separate from God, we are a part of Him, and He is a part of us. This means we are all one with each other. There have been times when I know God has sent me to give a message to someone who needed to hear it. Three of these events stand out in my mind. I usually have an envelope or envelopes in my car with money and a stone heart in them because I know God is going to have me come in contact with someone who needs not only the money but also a sign that He cares. One day I was sitting at a traffic light where a homeless man was standing. I opened my passenger window to give him an envelope. If the person looks at me, I always look directly into their eyes and say something like—May God be with you. This day I did that as I handed the man the envelope. He started to walk away and then turned back.

"You are an angel, aren't you?" he asked.

I said, "Yes."

To that he said, "You are surrounded by light!"

As the traffic light turned green, he turned and walked away. I know in my heart that man needed to feel God's love more than he needed the money. How wonderful it was that I was privileged to be God's messenger that day!

God's love came through me again on a cold Thursday afternoon in February. Snow was predicted for the weekend, which is unusual for this coastal Virginia city. On my way home from a meeting, I stopped by the liquor store. Standing outside the store was a man holding a cardboard sign that said he and his family were homeless and hungry and any money would be appreciated. This day, I happened to have an envelope in my bag that I had not yet transferred to my car. As I handed it to the man, a young man going into the store started yelling at me, "Don't give him anything! You will just encourage him!"

As I stepped into the vestibule behind this man, I said to his back, "I don't know if I want to come in here with your angry energy." But I did go in, and the man was standing inside the door waiting for me.

He was visibly shaking with anger and said, "I am building an apartment complex nearby, and I could give that man a full-time job. But he would rather stand out there and ask for money."

I asked him if he had told the man that. He answered, "Yes, many times."

This man followed me around the store, telling me why he was so angry. "I live in Virginia Beach," he said, "and there is one on every corner. They have a pimp who drops them off in the morning and picks them up in the afternoon. He takes a percentage of their take for the day."

I replied, "Yes, I know. I go to Virginia Beach often, and I have heard the same thing."

I then said, "But who am I to judge? It is not for me to judge whether or not someone is homeless and hungry."

Ignoring my comment, the man continued, "There was a man sitting outside the 7-Eleven where I went for coffee about five times a day. Every time I went in, I gave him a dollar. That was five dollars every day! Then one day I saw a man with a sign that said *DON'T GIVE THEM MONEY! IT WILL JUST ENCOURAGE THEM!"*

He then said, "Since reading that sign, I never again gave any one of them money."

I said, "I can see your viewpoint. Can you see mine?"

He did not answer me.

And I then said, "You work hard for your money, don't you?"

He replied an emphatic, "Yes! I work sixteen hours a day!"

When I glanced at the other customers in the store, I saw they were listening while trying to appear that they were not. But I stayed focused on the man, hearing what he had to say and answering him in a kind, calm, loving voice.

He was standing in line waiting to pay for his purchase when I said to him, "You know, you are a very handsome man."

He looked over at me and said, "Wow! Where did that come from?"

I could see all his anger dissipate, and I thought, *Yes, where did that come from?*

I did not know. Those words surprised me as much as they surprised him. But I answered him by saying, "I am just telling you what I see."

Then he said, "My girlfriend says I am better looking without my beard, but I tell her I work outside in the cold and the beard keeps my face warm."

What followed was a pleasant conversation between the two of us about beards. As he started to leave, he turned back to me and said, "Be safe."

I put two fingers to my lips, blowing him a kiss and said, "You be safe too."

Does that man ever think of our encounter? I do not know. What I do know is the man I saw leave the store that day was not the same man I saw go in. I was not the same person either. I had experienced the power of love.

It is exciting to me how God orchestrates things to come together. One day as I was driving home to Norfolk from Virginia Beach, I suddenly thought, *I think I will go to the bookstore*. I looked up to see where I was on the highway and realized I had to quickly get over if I was going to get off the correct exit. When I got to the bookstore, I decided to look for some greeting cards. I chose some and then thought I would go get a coffee in the café. I walked over to the café, and then thought, *I think I will go back and pay for these cards before I get my coffee*. There was one man ahead of me paying for his purchases, and as he did so he was complaining and complaining about how his wife was still looking around and he had to wait for her. As he finished paying and turned away, I was thinking, *Oh, get off it! Your wife has probably waited for you for half her life.*

That is what I was thinking.

So, I was shocked with what came out of my mouth. I do not normally call out to people in stores, but I called to him saying, "You are lucky to have someone to wait for!"

Where did that come from? It could only have come from God. I realized for some reason God had chosen me to give that man that message. The man chuckled when I said it, and I had no desire to say anything more.

After I paid for the cards and was walking back to the café, I saw him standing in the aisle watching and waiting for his wife. As you can see, I was not planning on going to the bookstore. Then when I got there, I was planning on getting a coffee before going to pay for my purchases. But obviously God had a different plan for me that day, and I listened to him. That is the thing I have learned—when I listen to those thoughts, inspirations, or intuitions, marvelous things happen!

Unfortunately, I do not always listen to my intuition when God is speaking to me. There are two parking spaces in my apartment parking lot that are angled toward each other because they are on a slight curve. Recently, I pulled into one of them and then looked across the way and thought, *I should move over there.* But did I listen? No!

I don't know what happened to me the next morning when I went to leave for an appointment. Instead of backing straight out—I was looking in my driver's side mirror trying to avoid the car next to me, but I somehow became confused and instead of avoiding it, I was getting closer and closer to it. Sometimes the angels send someone to help us, and I certainly needed them to send someone this day. By the time two young men came running over to help me, I appeared to be only inches away from the other car.

One of the men said, "You have already hit the car—so just back out and hit it again."

I said, "What?!"

I had to see for myself what I had done. I climbed over the console and got out the passenger's side door. Yes, I had made a mess of the other car's bumper. I got back into my car, climbed back over the console (thank goodness at seventy-five I can still do that).

I then cried, "What am I going to do? I'm trapped!"

The young man said, "Okay, listen to me, do what I say, and I will guide you out."

When I got out of the car to thank him, he started gesturing and saying, "Look at all this space you had! How did you do that?"

I looked him in the eyes and said, "I made a mistake."

The wonderful thing about the place I am in now is that I do not get upset about things. In the past, little things would throw me into a tailspin. Now, I can hit the car next to me and not get upset. When I get into my car, I always ask Archangel Michael to protect me, my car, and all those driving around me. Now I ask the parking lot angels to help me also—because obviously I need help parking and unparking.

When I got home that day, I called my insurance company. The woman gave me all the information for the claim, and I went and put it on the windshield of the damaged car with my name and phone number. I never heard from the owner of the car, but I saw she did have her car repaired. And I did not spend one minute being worried or upset. How wonderful is that? The Universe does take care of me—and it does help to have good insurance!

I was taking a weekend course recently given by three women who had been to India to become certified to offer the spiritual teachings of the Oneness University. I was the oldest of the eighteen participants. As I looked around the large circle, I saw so much pain. Many of the men and women were struggling with the things I had experienced in my life. As I looked at each one of them, I said, "I am older than all of you, and I have lived through these things that are causing you such pain. I want you to know there is peace and joy on the other side of your pain."

It really is a choice. I could wallow in pain because of Kelly's decision to not include me in her life. But instead, I am able to listen to my friends talk about their children and grandchildren. I can be happy for them when they show me the pictures of the weddings and graduations they attend. I do not focus on what I do not have. I look around and find joy in what I do have. That is not to say I never feel the pain. My grief does surface from time to time. I may feel it intensely. When that happens, I let myself feel it; I let the tears flow. I do not think grief ever completely disappears. It is there, but hopefully over time as we allow ourselves to feel the pain, it mitigates, never disappearing, only lessening so that we are able to feel the joy life holds for us.

Chapter 16

A Few Final Musings

I am so pleased to have shared my story with you. While most of it has been fun to write and has been written from a place of joy, there were sections that were quite difficult for me to revisit. They were so painful that I put off writing about them. They are things I no longer think about, but I had to in order for you to see and understand the full story of where I came from. I ask you to please join me in celebrating where I am today!

When I share my story, people often ask me how I am able to adopt such an optimistic attitude based upon everything that I lived through. In order to stay in a place of positive energy there are things I know I must do. I do not listen to or read the news. In fact, I do not own a television. There was nothing on it I wanted to watch, so I gave it away. I enjoy spending my evenings reading, writing, doing my art, and taking part in online spiritual classes. Some people I know watch the news all day. They tell me they are depressed, and when I ask them if they have ever thought about *not* watching the news, they say, "But I have to know what is going on." *Why?* Have you ever noticed that the news stories are the same over and over again? They are the same stories with different names and different places. If there is something important for me to know, I always learn about it. People are talking about it, and I hear it from them.

Almost every spiritual teacher stresses that one of the most important ways to connect to God is by meditating. I have found meditation to be a wonderful time to quiet my mind and connect with Spirit. This book came about through meditation. I had been told by three psychics that I would write a book—not that I *should* write a book, but that I *would* write a book. They told me, I listened, and that was the end of that. I did nothing about it until one day during meditation, I heard the Holy Spirit say, "Leslie, you have something important to say." And I immediately thought, *how can I ignore the Holy Spirit? I can't. I guess I am going to have to write a book!* At first, I wondered, *What am I going to write about?* Then I realized that if the Holy Spirit wanted me to write a book, He would also tell me what to say. You are reading what I started to write that day. Every day since that first day, I ask the Holy Spirit to help me write what *He* wanted me to say.

I also created a Committee of Writing Angels to assist me. On my committee is a mentor, an editor, a designer, and a coach. I asked my committee to include any other writing specialist they thought I might need. When I write, my committee is there with me along with the Holy Spirit. If I am having difficulty deciding how to word something, I will say, "I need help here" and the words begin to flow.

How wonderful my life is now that I no longer think I must do everything alone. I have tapped into the power of the Universe. Can you imagine how much power that is? The most exciting thing is that the Universe is made up of more spiritual beings than we can envision, and they are all here to help us, to guide us, and to protect us.

I have also learned that in order to keep my mind on positive things, I must put positive things into it. Gratitude and forgiveness are two things that are important if we want to change our way of being in the world. It is amazing how gratitude can almost instantly shift my negative feelings into positive ones. How can I feel unhappy when I am thinking about all the things I am grateful for? And by forgiving others and ourselves, we can remove the resentful feelings we have and replace them with feelings of love. Forgiveness and love are two of the greatest gifts we can give ourselves and others.

There is a list at the end of this book, where I share some of the inspirational spiritual teachers I have learned from. I have read their books and listened to them on YouTube. I have found that one teacher leads to another and then to another. You will find ones I have never heard of. Listen to the ones who resonate with you. When you learn to listen to your True Self, your inner guidance, you will know if what someone is saying is true for you. What is true for me may not be true for you. One thing I have found to be very powerful is to smile at myself when I am in front of a mirror. I look into my eyes and deeply connect with myself. It is interesting how differently I experience myself when I look into my eyes and smile. And I would not be here where I am without the angels. I have written about what the angels mean to me, how they have helped me in a myriad of ways, how they have protected me and led me to places I could only have dreamed of before I asked them into my life.

Years ago, I thought if I just read the "right" book, my depression would magically disappear. I read many books, but because there is nothing outside of us that will cure the pain, I was still depressed. Books can give us ideas and inspiration. Other people can *help* us, but it is an inside job.

We have to do the work.

And it *is* work.

It is not easy to change our way of being. It takes constant vigilance. We have to be determined to monitor our thoughts and our behavior in order to turn them into the positive instead of the negative. We have to be willing to feel the feelings that are connected to the painful things from our past. We cannot just talk about them—that is an intellectual exercise. Instead, we have to allow ourselves to *feel*. We heal when we connect the event to the feelings we did not let ourselves feel at the time and allow ourselves to feel them now. The wonderful thing is that there is joy on the other side of the pain and sorrow. Being able to live in the joy I live in now is worth every tear I shed. My eyelids may be wrinkled, but now there is a twinkle in my eyes!

I hope this book has inspired you and given you a few helpful ideas. In writing it, I felt as if I was talking to a good friend. Now that it is time to say goodbye, I know that I will miss you. I would like to leave you with a poem I wrote last year.

Because I Know

Because I know I am a Divine Idea in the Mind of God
I stand courageously in my truth.

I do not meld with the masses.

I can stand alone in the world of form
knowing I do not stand alone in the presence of God.

Listening to the Holy Spirit
I am filled with love.

When filled with love
there is no room for anger, fear, guilt or shame.

How can I be angry
when I stand surrounded by God's Peace?

How can I be afraid
when I stand firmly in God's Courage?

How can I feel guilt
when I am born of God's Perfection?

How can I feel shame
when I see myself through the Eyes of God?

Because I know
there is only God

I can be at peace in a world of chaos, fear and anger.

I can give love when love is not returned.

How can this not be so?

As God is I am.

With love and gratitude to all of you, dear readers,

Leslie Dyanne

PS: Most of all, cherish and nurture yourself, be kind and gentle and loving. Treat yourself as you would treat your beloved child or your lover or your very best friend.

I would love to hear from you. You can contact me at:

ldwhisperofthewind@gmail.com

My website is lesliedyanne.com

Poetic Works
By Leslie Dyanne

Two Strong Women

You sobbed in my arms for hours
mascara running down your cheeks.

Your lashes made two black caterpillars on my pants
when you threw your face onto my lap.

I thought I knew all the horrors of your past.

But who can truly know another's sorrow?

You sobbed in my arms for hours.

Your words tumbling out on top of each other
told me things no one should ever have to share.

How do we stay strong in the presence of such pain?

Hidden Scars

They say the definition of *battering* is
repeated physical abuse.

When he has an affair and comes home and says
sex is so much better with her than it is with you.

What do you call that?

And what would you call it when he says
making love to you is like making love to a
dead person?

The only way I know you are
alive is I can hear your heart beat.

BEAT! BEAT! BEAT!

I call it a *battering* of the heart.

Where are the scars, you ask?

The scars are hidden, but they throb in the night.

They scream with pain and anger and hopelessness.

Are these scars not real because you cannot see them?

The scar above my eye is very faint now.

But the pain in my heart may never go away.

When I wrote this poem, I thought the pain would never go away,
but I can tell you now that it does. If you want to heal, you can. You
are far stronger than you realize. The pain does not magically disappear. One must be determined to live a different way. Never feel
shame. No one ever deserves to be abused. You are so very loved!

Beautiful Things

You tell me about your friend
and her handsome husband.

She was hemorrhaging.

He went out for his run
before taking her to the emergency room.

Oh, I say, he is an abuser.

No, he can't be.

He buys her beautiful things.

Why, he even bought her a fur coat.

I bet it wasn't the kind of fur she wanted, I say.

You look at me, surprised.

How did you know?

This is a conversation I actually had with a woman. Often, this is
how an abuser operates. He wants the outside world to think he is a
great guy, but he is not going to give her what *she* wants.

Silenced

Shamed by his laughter.
Scorned by his look.
I believed I had no voice.
And for years I was silent.

Who Am I?

You thought you had nothing to say.

But the words will not stop
as the tears would not stop.

Take the words to go out into the world
and find out who you are and where you are.

Is this the planet Earth?

Where have I been all these years?

Living under a rock?

Yes, in the dark under a rock.

Memories

I throw away things
give them away
sell them on eBay.

Other people take photographs
buy souvenirs.

They want to remember.

Not I.

My memories haunt me
attack me when I am unaware.

I don't want things to remind me.

*   *   *

Let's take a walk down memory lane.

No, thank you very much.

I'd rather not go that way.

I think I'll take this path instead.

Rules

Pummeling us with rules
our mothers prepared us for life.

Armed with Do's and Don'ts
we went out into the world.

It wasn't until our lives started to fall apart
that we began to question.

Who made up these rules?
Where did they come from?

*   *   *

Take the rules
hold them in your hands
turn them over

Do they say: Made in China?

Sharon's Choice

You always sat in the back of the room

Alone.

A beautiful woman wrapped in a cloak of sadness.

What made you come sit next to me that day?

Of all the people there
why was I the one you chose to share your pain?

As a young girl you had a dog.

You loved your dog
and she loved you.

She waited for your bus each day
slept with you at night.

One day, your father came to you and said:

If you let me take your dog away, I will buy you a horse.

Many agonizing days and sleepless nights followed.

How could you give your beloved dog away?

She was your friend
your constant companion.

But as your father knew
you had always wanted a horse.

You wanted a horse of your very own
a horse you could ride
a horse you could love.

Finally, you told your father

Yes, take my dog and bring me a horse.

You watched your father lead her away
a big man with a little dog.

That night, he came home with a horse
a small plastic horse.

Your father took your beloved dog away
and in return he gave you a dime store horse.

It has been years since you told me your story
and I weep for you still.

But on that day
all I could do for you was listen.

This is a true story, and it is still hard for me to even think about. It tells
me that cruelty and abuse have no limits. Let us combat the cruelty in
the world with love. Love is the most powerful thing there is.

The Dreamer

I often dream of houses
beautiful houses, elegant in their simplicity.

Created by my untethered imagination
they are at once strange and familiar.

These are dreams of wonder
full of surprises.

I find rooms I never knew existed
filled with lost and forgotten possessions.

Looking out a window
I see the house is on the water
with a magnificent view.

These dreams are uplifting
empowering dreams.

I awake with a longing.

I yearn to have a safe place
with secret rooms holding unexpected treasures.

If everything one dreams is part of the dreamer
then I am the house.

What a glorious thought!

Do I have unexplored places
creative gifts unknown even to me, the dreamer?

The Box

Where are you? I can't see you.

Of course not. I am an expert at being invisible.
It is safer to be invisible.

No, where are you?

I am trying to fit into this box.

What are you doing in that box?

Look inside and you will see me.
I am all scrunched up attempting to be what everyone else
wants me to be.

Why do you care what others want?
Each person is going to want you to be
something different. Don't you know you are only meant
to be who you are?

Never listen to what others say.
No one else knows more about you than you do.
In fact, you are the only one who knows anything about you.
And unless you look at yourself through the eyes of God, you are
not seeing who you truly are.

But who am I? I have been in this box so long I don't
know who I am.

Come on! Get out of the box and we can figure that out together.

But it feels safer here.
It takes courage to stand alone, declaring who I am,
what I want, what I am willing to do, what I refuse to do.
People will turn their backs on me if I don't stay in this box.

Yes, some will, but others won't. Then you will meet people
who love you for who you are. Wouldn't you rather be
loved for who you are instead of being loved (if you can call it
that) for being the person someone else thinks you should be?

Good heavens, get out of that box!
You are meant to fly like an eagle, bloom like a rose,
rise like the sun, sing like the nightingale!
Don't you know you can fall like the rain, crash like the waves,
howl like the wind?

You really have forgotten there is so much more of you than what
is in that box. Haven't you?

Yes, I guess I have. I have been inside here so long.

Climb out and stretch. Stretch your arms. Stretch your legs.
Stretch your mind. Let it go. Let it fly on the wind like a kite.
A kite may be tethered to the ground, but at the same time
it lets go and the wind takes it places it never knew
existed. It soars. It dips until it almost touches the
ground before shooting straight up and streaking right toward
the sun.

Wouldn't you rather be like the kite than crouched in
that box?

Please get out of the box. There is so much more for you out
here. Don't you want to smell the jasmine on the cool
evening breeze, float down the river with the sun on your face,
write a poem, dance to the music? There are no limits to what
you can do or who you can be.

Okay, you have convinced me. I will get out.
Don't look though.

Why not? You are beautiful no matter where you are
or where you have been—even with the imprint of that
box on your face.

Stretch, feel, smell, touch, live. Live, I say. You cannot
live hiding in a box.

Let's burn your box and watch the smoke carry away
all your angry thoughts, all your bitter thoughts, all your
judgmental thoughts, all your limiting thoughts, all your thoughts
of what others may think, all your fears, all your worries.

As the smoke dissipates, you will be free, free to be. Just be. That is all you have to do. Just be beautiful, wonderful, magnificent you!

My Grateful Acknowledgments

I am so very fortunate to have each and every one of these women in my life. Possessions have never been important to me. I have always said it is the people in my life that matter the most. And with these women I have been extremely blessed. I thank each and every one of you for believing in me and sharing in my excitement about this, my first book.

First, it is with deep gratitude that I want to thank Marci Shimoff for writing the foreword. Marci's book *Happy for No Reason* greatly inspired me, and I am honored by her beautiful words in the foreword to my book. Thank you, Marci!

Without Marci Shimoff, Dr. Sue Morter and Lisa Garr and their Year of Miracles course, I would not be writing this today. Through their program I was connected to a wonderful coach, Leila Reyes. During our first coaching session, Leila asked me, "Would you like to speak to a publisher about your book?"

Now, how could I say no to that! Leila emailed Michelle Vandepas, the cofounder of GracePoint Publishing, to introduce me. Michelle and I spent days trying to connect with each other. In that time, I decided to send her the title, dedication page, and introduction to the book, so when we talked, she would have an idea of what I was writing. When we finally spoke by phone, Michelle explained the publishing world to me and said they would like to have me in their program, and she knew the perfect coach for me—Shauna Hardy. And Shauna was perfect for me! It was magical working with her. Next, I was blessed to have the privilege of working with developmental editor, Amy Delcambre. She worked hard with me honing the book into what it is today.

Through good times and bad, my sister Deborah Keegan has been there for me. Linda Lighthill became her partner twenty-eight years ago and joined Deborah in supporting me in so many ways.

Kimberly Benton and I met in college thirty years ago when I was in my forties and she was in her twenties. We have been dear friends ever since. She is the kind of friend with whom I can honestly share my deepest, and sometimes darkest, secrets.

Some people say you cannot make new friends when you are older, but Dana Walker and I fractured that myth when we met. I was seventy and she was sixty-eight. I call her my cheerleader because she has always loved my art and my writing. I must give Dana a special thank you for the meticulous editing she did to make sure my book was ready to go out into the world.

Another dear friend I have made in the last couple of years is Cindy Lyn Lee. One of the most wonderful things about my relationship with each of these women is our laughter. For me, there is no substitute for laughter.

I am fortunate to have found a marvelous counselor, Pamela Hopkins, who has taught me how to keep a positive outlook on life. She has been instrumental in helping me move from sometimes living in joy to almost always being there. Visiting with Patti Somers who works in Pamela's office is one of the highlights of my week.

Pamela introduced me to Amanda Aksel who has been my coach, encouraging me through the last edits of the book. And most exciting of all, she designed my beautiful website! Thank you, Amanda!

The Year of Miracles gave me three wonderful Miracle Sisters—Laura, Tricia, and Paige. When we meet on Zoom every other week, we cheer each other's wins and miracles. Between our meetings, we stay connected by text, supporting each other by sending uplifting messages and love. Laura, Tricia, and Paige have encouraged me throughout the process of birthing this book, culminating in being its beta readers. Thank you, Miracle Sisters!

I have a fun group of friends here in the apartment building where I live. As soon as I moved in, I was greeted by them and asked to join their book club. We now play Rummikub every Friday afternoon. And if the young people in the building could hear our silliness and laughter, they would realize there is no age limit on having fun!

With love in my heart for each and every one of you!

Leslie Dyanne

2025

Resources

BOOKS

These are just a few of the books that have helped me along the way, in the 1990s when I was going through my divorce and then as I have been traveling my spiritual journey.

Alan Cohen, *A Course in Miracles: Mastering the Journey from Fear to Love*

Alice Miller, *The Drama of the Gifted Child: The Search for the True Self**

> **The Gifted Child* is everyone who has survived childhood abuse.

Don Miguel Ruiz, *The Four Agreements***

> **Ruiz says if you follow these agreements, it will change your life. It is true. They will.

Esther and Jerry Hicks, *The Law of Attraction: The Basic of the Teachings of Abraham*

Jean Jenson, MSW, *Reclaiming Your Life: A Step-by-Step Guide to Using Regression Therapy to Overcome the Effects of Childhood Abuse****

> ***My wonderful psychiatrist, Dr. P, said if he had to save one book in his library, this would be it.

Kenneth Wapnick, PhD, *The Healing Power of Kindness, Volume One: Releasing Judgement*

Kenneth Wapnick, PhD, *The Healing Power of Kindness, Volume Two: Forgiving Our Limitations*

Marianne Williamson, A Return to Love

Marci Shimoff with Carol Kline, *Happy for No Reason: 7 Steps to Being Happy from the Inside Out*

Marci Shimoff with Carol Kline, *Love for No Reason: 7 Steps to Creating a Life of Unconditional Love*

Mike Dooley, *Infinite Possibilities*

Neale Donald Walsch, *Conversations with God, Books One Through Four*

Pat Rodegast and Judith Stanton, *Emmanuel's Book*

Pat Rodegast and Judith Stanton, *Emmanuel's Book III*

SQuire Rushnell, *When God Winks at You: How God Speaks Directly to You Through the Power of Coincidence*

Tama Kieves, *Thriving Through Uncertainty: Moving Beyond Fear of the Unknown and Making Change Work for You*

On YouTube:

Esther and Abraham Hicks. Esther channels Abraham who helps us see how to get into and stay in a positive mindset. Abraham has a wonderful sense of humor, and I find his speaking through Esther to be delightful to listen to.

Father Richard Rohr is a Franciscan friar who founded the Center for Action and Contemplation in Albuquerque, New Mexico. Although I have read many of his books, they are a little too deep for me to fully understand, but listening to him on YouTube is an entirely different experience. I have learned so much from him about being a spiritual person.

Suzanne Giesemann is a Messenger of Hope and the founder and teacher of The Awakened Way—a path to knowing who you are and why you are here.

This is just to get you started. As you begin listening to speakers on YouTube you will be led to others that interest you. I found Father Richard while listening to Abraham Hicks.

About the Author

Not everyone is told by the Holy Spirit to write a book, but that is how *I Am the Whisper of the Wind* came into being. I had written what I call social issue poems for many years, but I had never written much prose. I did not have a desire to write a book so when three different psychics told me that was what I was going to do, I ignored each one of them. Then one day in meditation, the Holy Spirit said to me, "Leslie, you have something important to say." I immediately sat down and started to write because how could I ignore the Holy Spirit? As I wrote, I realized I did have something important to say. For years I did not like the word HOPE because I felt it kept women in abusive relationships, always hoping their partner would change. But as I wrote, I began to see HOPE in a different way. I knew I wanted to share my story in order to give women the courage to change themselves, to know they can take charge of their lives. I wanted to be an example of how one can go from being a depressed abused woman to being one who lives freely in a life of happiness and joy.

I Am the Whisper of the Wind is not a self-help or how-to book. It is the narrative of my life. As I wrote it, I felt as if I was telling the story to a dear friend. Change is not easy, but I wanted to show how it is possible. It was not until I was seventy years old that I began to get in touch with the spiritual part of me and in so doing I learned how the power of the Universe is always available to guide and support me. It has been my desire that my words will inspire the readers of my book to discover this at a younger age and have more years to live peacefully with themselves and others, knowing they are divinely loved by a multitude of Heavenly Beings.

I am currently writing my second book titled *Call on the Angels, Damn It*. Yes, the angels gave the title to me, and I could imagine them laughing as they did so! When I am not writing, I am reading. Books have always been the companions that have helped me survive my life. I have one with me wherever I go. I am also a life-time doodler, and I have taken my doodling to a higher level and turned it into art.

LeslieDyanne.com

For more great books from Empower Press
Visit Books.GracePointPublishing.com

EMP⊙WER
P   R   E   S   S

If you enjoyed reading *I Am the Whisper of the Wind,* and purchased it
through an online retailer, please return to the site and write a review to help
others find the book.

www.ingramcontent.com/pod-product-compliance
Lightning Source LLC
Chambersburg PA
CBHW070120100426
42744CB00010B/1878